Fund Raising

William F. Stier, Jr., Ph.D.

Made E-Z

MADE E-Z PRODUCTS™ Inc.
Deerfield Beach, Florida / www.MadeE-Z.com

Fund Raising Made E-Z™
Dr. William F. Stier, Jr.

Limited warranty and disclaimer

This self-help product is intended to be used by the consumer for his/her own benefit. It may not be reproduced in whole or in part, resold or used for commercial purposes without written permission from the publisher. In addition to copyright violations, the unauthorized reproduction and use of this product to benefit a second party may be considered the unauthorized practice of law.

This product is designed to provide authoritative and accurate information in regard to the subject matter covered. However, the accuracy of the information is not guaranteed, as laws and regulations may change or be subject to differing interpretations. Consequently, you may be responsible for following alternative procedures, or using material or forms different from those supplied with this product. It is strongly advised that you examine the laws of your state before acting upon any of the material contained in this product.

As with any matter, common sense should determine whether you need the assistance of an attorney. We urge you to consult with an attorney, qualified estate planner, or tax professional, or to seek any other relevant expert advice whenever substantial sums of money are involved, you doubt the suitability of the product you have purchased, or if there is anything about the product that you do not understand including its adequacy to protect you. Even if you are completely satisfied with this product, we encourage you to have your attorney review it.

Neither the author, publisher, distributor nor retailer are engaged in rendering legal, accounting or other professional services. Accordingly, the publisher, author, distributor and retailer shall have neither liability nor responsibility to any party for any loss or damage caused or alleged to be caused by the use of this product.

Copyright notice

The purchaser of this guide is hereby authorized to reproduce in any form or by any means, electronic or mechanical, including photocopying, all forms and documents contained in this guide, provided it is for non-profit, educational or private use. Such reproduction requires no further permission from the publisher and/or payment of any permission fee.

The reproduction of any form or document in any other publication intended for sale is prohibited without the written permission of the publisher. Publication for nonprofit use should provide proper attribution to Made E-Z Products™.

Table of contents

DEDICATION

To my wife, Veronica Ann, and our five children—Mark, Missy, Michael, Patrick, and Will, III—for their loving encouragement and continued unselfish support.

A special thanks also to Samantha, Katie Lee, Joshua, Michael, Jessica, Bree, and Jackson William.

About the author

Dr. William F. Stier, Jr. is an international expert in fundraising and promotions for sport, recreation and non-profit organizations. He currently directs the undergraduate program in sport management and the graduate athletic administration program at the State University of New York, Brockport, where he also has responsibility for the undergraduate sport coaching program. While at SUNY, he has also assumed the positions of director of intercollegiate athletics (1983-1990) and chairperson of the physical education and sport department (1983-1986). During 1992-1993, he served as president of the faculty senate, and in the fall of 1994, he was appointed graduate director.

A frequent speaker on fundraising and promotions for non-profit organizations, Dr. Stier has made 157 international professional presentations at international (56), national (57), regional (17), and state (27) professional conferences and conventions. On the international level, Dr. Stier was one of five sports scholars invited by the United States Olympic Committee to speak at the international Olympic Academy in Olympia, Greece. He has also been invited to conduct administrative workshops and sports clinics and served as a management consultant in Singapore, Mexico, St. Kitts-Nevis, Hong Kong, Canada, Taiwan and Malaysia. He spent a sabbatical serving as Special Assistant to the President and visiting professor at the National School for Sports Coaches [Escuela Nacional de Deportiva] in México City. While in México he also taught as a visiting professor at the Escuela Superior Educación Física [Superior Physical Education School].

A prolific writer, Dr. Stier has authored more than 224 scholarly articles in 61 international (8), national (189), regional (1), and state (26) professional publications. He is currently the editor of the national refereed journal, The Physical Educator and also the editor of the International Journal of Sport Management.

Dr. Stier has also served on the editorial boards and/or the advisory review panels of nine international and national professional journals, including *(1) International Journal of Sport Management; (2) Sport Marketing Quarterly; (3) Athletic Management; (4) Applied Research in Coaching and Athletics Annual; (5) Journal of the International Council for Health, Physical Education, Recreation, Sport, and Dance; (6) Journal of Physical Education, Recreation and Dance; (7) The Physical Educator; (8) ERIC Digest;* and *(9) Strategies.*

Twelve of Dr. Stier's recent publications include eleven books *(1) Sport Management—Career Planning and Professional Preparation; (2) Successful Sport Fund Raising; (3) Fund Raising for Sport and Recreation; (4) More Fantastic Fund Raising for Sport and Recreation, (5) Successful Coaching—Strategies and Tactics; (6) Coaching Modern Basketball—Hints, Strategies & Tactics; (7) Coaching: Concepts & Practices; (8) Athletic Administration: Policies, Procedures and Practices; (9) Administering Universities' and Colleges' Admissions Offices: Policies, Practices & Procedures; (10) Problem-Solving for Coaches, (11) The Management of Sport, Recreation and Fitness Programs: Concepts and Practices;* and, *(12) a monograph—Alternative Career Paths in Physical Education: Sport Management.* This is the twelfth book that Dr. Stier has authored in the areas of fund raising, sport and administration/management.

Honored by his peers on numerous occasions, he received the first annual "Sport Management Achievement Award" by the Sport Management Council of the National Association of Sport and Physical Education in 1999. In addition, he has been recognized as Researcher of the Year on two occasions within New York state and received the Merit Award in Physical Education twice by the Eastern District Association of Health, Physical Education, Recreation and Dance.

In 1985, he was inducted as a Research Fellow within the Research Consortium of the American Alliance for Health, Physical Education, Recreation and Dance (AAHPERD).

Dr. Stier is a member of the National Speakers' Bureau of the National Association of Girls and Women in Sports and has had several weekly TV shows, including *The Bill Stier Show,* Rochester, New York, dealing with current sport topics. Dr. Stier is listed in the Marquis *Who's Who in America; Who's Who in American Education, Who's Who In International Education,* and is a member of the American Alliance for Health, Physical Education, Recreation and Dance; the National Association for Girls and Women in Sports; the National Association for Sport and Physical Education; and, the North American Society for Sport Management.

Introduction to Fund Raising Made E-Z™

The book you now hold in your hand, *Fund Raising Made E-Z*, presents 75 top fund raising projects. Each of these fundraisers can be implemented by people just like you. They are presented in a practical and user-friendly format, accompanied by concepts and suggestions which are very helpful in solving the ever present problem of generating resources for sport, recreation and other non-profit organizations.

The author is an internationally recognized expert in the art and science of fund raising and promotions. In addition to speaking extensively throughout the United States as well as overseas, Dr. Stier has also written extensively about fund raising, promotion and sport programs. If you wish to generate much needed financial support as well as enthusiasm and positive public relations for a wide range of non-profit entities, including sport, recreation and leisure programs—this book was designed with you in mind. In it you find a variety of different and distinct techniques and tactics to help you and your organization generate funds. Thus, whether you are a novice or have a wealth of experience in the area of fund raising, this book can be of real help to you and your organization.

This book is based upon proven, successful fund raising concepts. Throughout the publication fund raising guidelines and suggestions are clearly illustrated which, if followed, should be of real practical help to those individuals facing the formidable task of generating additional money and support for sport or recreation organizations, as well as other non-profit entities.

Now that the 21st century is upon us, there continues to be an ever increasing need for outside fund raising, especially for non-profit organizations which are faced with insufficient operating budgets. As a result, sport, recreation and leisure organizations will continue to have great need for individuals who are knowledgeable in the art and science of fund raising and are capable of meeting the challenges of generating additional financial support. This is especially important with limited traditional sources of funding.

The fund raising plans outlined herein include projects that have been successfully used by a variety of recreation and sport organizations—both large and small—to generate additional and much needed resources and support (financial and public relations) for their programs. The purpose of this book is to provide you, the would-be as well as the experienced fundraiser, with the where-with-all to actually plan, organize, assess and implement successful fund raising projects, in light of available resources as well as current limitations or existing restrictions.

The need for individuals who are knowledgeable and skilled in fund raising has never been greater than today. With less and less money available for organizations through the regular budgetary process, there is an ever increasing need for outside fund raising and promotional activities. Today, individuals in almost every sport and recreation organization and educational institution are finding themselves financially pinched and in need of additional resources. The challenge continues for those of you involved in sport and recreational organizations and other non-profit entities to generate sufficient resources in a timely fashion to support worthwhile activities.

This includes administrators and recreation leaders; individuals responsible for fund raising for various non-profit, social organizations such as the Boy Scouts, Girl Scouts, YMCA/YWCAs, Jewish Community Centers, Catholic Youth Organizations, and Boys Clubs of America; coaches and athletic administrators of youth sport teams such as Little League baseball, soccer teams, midget football squads and youth hockey organizations; booster club members for youth sport and for junior and senior high sports; and, of course, coaches and athletic administrators at junior and senior high schools, junior colleges, and four-year colleges and universities. In fact, the author received significant assistance from many individuals representing these and other non-profit organizations.

Specifically written for sport, recreation and non-profit practitioners who find themselves out on the firing line seeking fund raising ideas for their respective organizations, this primer provides very specific and helpful ideas and plans for conducting fund raising projects and activities. In these pages are practical ideas and suggestions on how to successfully plan and implement any number of successful fund raising projects that can generate money and enhance the image of the program.

Some readers may be able to simply lift some fund raising projects directly from this book and implement them in their own communities with few, if any, significant changes. Other fund raising projects, however, might require either moderate or substantial alterations and adaptations in order to be successfully implemented for your particular situation. Thus, this book is similar to a cookbook in that the various fund raising projects and ideas may be viewed as recipes which, if followed even with some changes, will enable you to plan and implement highly successful and satisfying fund raising events to suit your own tastes and preferences.

Every fund raising situation is somewhat different, perhaps even unique. The key to successfully conducting any single fund raising project is to find out what will work in your own particular situation. Different organizations have differing circumstances or parameters which dictate what can and cannot be accomplished or even attempted. You, the fundraiser, must come to terms with what is possible to do in the realm of fund raising and promotion in terms of your own situation and circumstances, including existing limitations, restrictions as well as identifiable assets and advantages.

These 75 fund raising projects can also be used as a foundation from which you devise your own unique fund raising projects to satisfy your particular needs. The contents of this book are organized so that you will learn what you must do to plan, organize, implement, assess and bring to closure an effective and efficient fund raising event that is financially profitable and that creates positive public relations. This book helps you to better understand the concepts, processes and tasks involved in generating money as well as promoting your program and enhancing the image of your program.

This book is divided into six sections. The initial part explains how to best use this book while providing insight into basic fund raising theories and principles. This section also provides specific suggestions and guidelines for conducting successful fund raising events. The second section includes a helpful "Fundraiser Finder" which serves as an index to the 75 fund raising projects included within this book. It categorizes and summarizes each of the projects based upon the net profit that can be expected to be raised, the complexity of the event, the number of people needed and the amount of seed money required to initiate the event. The remaining four sections of the book deal with the fundraisers (projects) themselves. The fundraisers are categorized into one of the four sections based upon their potential net profit, the amount that you might reasonably expect to generate.

Material presented for each fund raising project includes all of the information you need to plan, organize, implement, and conclude the event. This information includes an explanation and a detailed description of the project; the potential cash income and other benefits in light of the time, money and effort expended; suggestions about when to plan and hold the event; time requirements to plan, organize and implement the project; the degree of complexity or difficulty of the activity; the resources needed in terms of facilities, seed money, equipment and supplies; possible publicity and related promotional activities; staffing and personnel requirements;

information about any necessary permits or licenses; tips for managing potential legal, financial and public relations risks; and additional specific hints for the ultimate success of the project.

The information concerning specific projects as well as the general fund raising principles in Chapter 1 (*Using This Book Effectively*) enable you to accomplish three objectives: First, you can develop a basic understanding of the elements necessary for making any fund raising project a success—the fundamentals of fund raising.

Second, you learn how to apply this basic knowledge, coupled with your own ideas and your understanding of your own needs and resources, to plan effective and efficient fund raising activities. And, third, you learn how to actually implement your plans for fund raising into highly successful projects. It is this pragmatic presentation of fund raising theory combined with the practical suggestions, strategies, hints, and ideas that makes this book of unique value to organizers of the fund raising events in the world of sport, recreation, and other non-profit organizations. I wish you much luck as you enter the fascinating world of fund raising, promotions and public relations.

Using this book effectively 1

Chapter 1

Using this book effectively

What you'll find in this chapter:

⇒ The four major objectives of an event

⇒ Resources worth considering for any event

⇒ Insight into event risk management

⇒ Considerations for events serving alcohol

⇒ Special considerations including licensing

Although sport and recreation have never been more popular in this country, this popularity has not come without a price. Accompanying this tremendous increase in participation has been an increase in the cost of providing and conducting meaningful sport and recreational activities. Leaders and practitioners alike, recreation specialists, coaches, and sport administrators are all too painfully aware of the financial challenge facing almost all organizations that provide sport and recreation programs. This is true whether such activities are provided within the structure of an educational setting, a youth sport organization, a recreation department, or some other non-profit entity.

The financial needs of sport and recreation programs must effectively be met if these programs are to continue to exist and thrive, if they are to meet the needs of the individuals and communities that they serve. Without adequate funding, sport and recreation programs, whatever their intrinsic value, are probably doomed to failure. Thus, securing financial support is rapidly being recognized as one of the prime responsibilities (and challenges) facing recreation leaders, sport administrators, and athletic coaches.

In today's society, the ability to effectively and efficiently secure adequate funding is considered an essential, indispensable skill in the operation of any sport, educational or recreation program. The person who is a competent and successful fundraiser is viewed as an invaluable asset to any organization. As a result, fund raising has become commonplace, a fact of life, for those of us in such programs.

There are four major objectives for any successful fund raising event. First, it must be financially successful. That is, the effort generates additional resources that may be used to facilitate your organization's numerous useful and worthwhile activities. Second, the fund raising project or event generates genuine enthusiasm for the fund raising effort itself. Third, the positive image and perception of your organization or program is reinforced and even enhanced as a result of the fund raising project's extensive exposure, publicity, and public relations. Fourth, truly successful fund raising projects and efforts creates and reinforces real support for the on-going efforts as well as the goals of the sponsoring organization.

No two fund raising situations are identical. Planners in one community will find that their situations are usually somewhat different, sometimes radically different, from situations in other communities. The differences can be in any number of different areas. For example, resources (facilities, personnel, equipment, supplies, publicity outlets, promotional techniques, money, etc.) may be lacking or not available in some communities while in others they are abundant. Additionally, there could be other types of limitations related to finances, programs, public relations, perceptions, image, reputation, competition, and location that could serve as restrictions or limitations on your efforts to generate outside resources through fund raising.

Thus, I encourage you to look at each of the fund raising projects from a discriminating and critical perspective. See if the ideas and suggestions presented in the book can help in the implementation of each project. The objective is to determine for yourself what will work and what will not work in your own organization and in your own community. And, you must make this critical decision while keeping in mind the availability of resources as well as any limitations that might exist as well.

I hope that as you read through the 75 fund raising projects presented in this book you begin to develop a clear understanding of the similarities as well as the differences between the different types and methods of fund raising. It is important to remember that many projects in the book contain information and suggestions that are applicable to other fund raising efforts also found in the book.

Therefore, carefully examine each of the projects that use similar or related fund raising concepts. For example, if you are thinking of having a fund raising project involving sales then it might be helpful to read all of the fund raising projects that use the sales technique. Similarly, there are several fund raising efforts that revolve around the concept of gambling. And there are several activities that are based on athletic contests and the use of food. If you read each of the fund raising projects based upon the same or similar concept you will be able to improve your understanding of the fund raising process. The end result should be an improvement in terms of your ability to create, plan and carry out a highly successful fund raising program.

How this book is structured

The Appendix section features a helpful tool called the *Fundraiser Finder.* This chart helps you quickly select an appropriate fundraiser that might be appropriate and possible for your own organization. In the *Fundraiser Finder,* each of the 75 fund raising projects is listed (alphabetically) and is assigned a number. To the right of each fundraiser are listed (1) the potential dollar profit, (2) the complexity of the event, (3) the number of people who should be involved in planning and implementing the project, (4) the amount of money needed to initially finance the fundraiser, and (5) the page number in the book where the project is described in full.

Each of the different fund raising projects included in the book are provided in an identical format so that they are easily understood and so that you can quickly compare one project with another. Within each project, information is presented in terms of the following elements:

Potential net income

This is an estimated net profit that can be expected for each fund raising project. Since profits can vary with the event and the community in light of any number of factors, the figures provided are only estimates.

Complexity/degree of difficulty

Each project is rated in terms of complexity: low, moderate, and high. These words indicate the general amount of work, effort and time involved in planning, organizing and carrying out the project. Naturally, the complexity of any event depends upon the sponsoring organization's resources, priorities, goals, limitations, competition, restrictions, and community climate. What might not be difficult for one group might indeed be difficult for another.

Description

This section explains the essence of the project. A succinct explanation is presented of the details of the event that must be addressed if it is to be successful. Naturally, you need to account for unique circumstances within your organization and in your community when planning, organizing, and implementing any fundraiser.

Scheduling

Suggestions are provided regarding the best time(s) of the year when the individual fund raising effort may be initiated. This information includes techniques and strategies for successful event scheduling.

Resources

This is a general heading that includes six distinct categories that describe various resources (assets, tools, etc.) that are required for the successful implementation of the specific fund raising project. The categories of resources include the following:

- **Facilities**—This category describes the facilities, if any, that are required to carry out the project. Suggestions, when appropriate, are also provided regarding possible location(s) of facilities.

- **Equipment and supplies**—Most fund raising efforts involve some type of equipment and supplies. Those items deemed necessary or appropriate are listed, and suggestions are included on how you can obtain and best utilize such items, preferably at reduced or no cost.

- **Publicity and promotion**—A variety of suggestions regarding the use of publicity and promotional tactics are presented for each fund raising project. The timing of such promotional efforts is discussed, when appropriate. The general public should be aware that the fund raising project is being sponsored by a worthy non-profit organization. Don't hesitate to publicize how the profits will be used within the community.

- **Time**—Information is presented concerning time requirements, both for the actual event as well as for the planning and implementation stages.

- **Expenditures**—In many instances, it costs money to make money. This information will give you an idea of how much money you might have to spend, and for what, in order to conduct the fundraiser. Usually you should try to avoid spending money whenever possible. Instead try to obtain tools, assets, and resources for free, at cost, or at least at a significantly reduced cost. Every dollar not spent is a dollar earned. If you need poster boards, ask for donations. If signs need to be painted, find someone who will donate time and expertise.

  Of course, money will have to be spent in many projects. When fund raising projects involve the selling of items, organizers frequently will need to buy (at reduced cost, naturally) those items that are to be sold; this is part of the cost of sales. Note that there is no magic formula or fixed percentage that you can use as a benchmark in determining how much money should be spent to raise a specific dollar amount. Naturally, the less money spent the better. But the amount will depend upon your specific situation and the existing circumstances in which you find yourself.

- **Personnel (staff/volunteers)**—No fund raising project is possible without people behind the effort. Personnel includes both paid staff of the sponsoring organization as well as volunteers or boosters. Under this category are suggestions relating to the approximate number of people who should be involved with different aspects of the event. Additionally, a description of their principal responsibilities and tasks is provided. Frequently, there are influential individuals (Centers of Influence) within any community who can open doors to potential contributors and organizations on behalf of the fund raising organization. Identifying and taking advantage of these centers of influence is all too often the key to conducting a successful fund raising effort.

Risk management

This section provides insight into ways to avoid risks. Fundraisers need to be concerned with legal risks, such as liability concerns and insurance matters, as well as financial risks that could prove disastrous. There are also public relations risks that the organizers need to be well aware of lest they end up with "egg on their faces." The phrase Risk Management also suggests that one should examine worst-case scenarios in an effort to make appropriate and timely plans to avoid or minimize, as much as possible, such negative consequences.

Permits/licenses

This category provides suggestions relative to securing of permits, licenses, and even permissions that may be necessary if you are to successfully implement the fund raising project. When appropriate, information is provided in terms of where specific permits or licenses might be obtained.

Hints

This category is reserved for specific suggestions to help you plan, execute, and evaluate the fund raising event. Additionally, insight into alternative ways to conduct the specific event is provided. You should take these hints with a grain of salt, so to speak, in light of individual resources and limitations in your community and within the sponsoring group itself.

Gambling and games of chance

It is important that individuals involved in fund raising take special care when planning and implementing fund raising efforts that involve gambling or games of chance. Some states, counties and communities have laws or ordinances either prohibiting or restricting games of chance and gambling activities. Using games of chance or gambling projects as part of a fundraiser without securing the appropriate permits or licenses, when such are required, can result in serious legal and punitive actions against you as well as against the sponsoring organization. Prudent fundraisers meet all legal obligations. It is important to never expose yourself or your organization to potential legal action by assuming law enforcement agencies may overlook the lack of a permit.

Those fund raising organizers who abide by the philosophy of "forgiveness is easier to obtain than permission" need to be aware of the possible negative consequences of illegally conducting gambling activities. These consequences can be severe in terms of not only legal penalties but also negative publicity and tarnished image. The best course is to check with your organization's legal counsel first.

The state of New York, for instance, requires that organizations wishing to conduct such games must secure *advance permission* from both the New York State Racing and Wagering Board and from the local municipality (through the town clerk) where the event will take place. In fact, there are two kinds of permits, one for bingo and one for games of chance, that are available in New York. Bingo games cost the sponsoring organization $18.75 per event. Permits for games of chance cost $25 per day. An additional requirement is that a financial statement must be submitted to the state within a specified number of days following the event.

Alcoholic beverages

Alcoholic beverages may be served at fund raising events, but organizers are required to first secure the necessary state and/or local liquor licenses or permits, which vary among locales. Some jurisdictions require one specific permit for hard liquor (scotch, whiskey, vodka, gin, etc.) and another for light spirits (beer, wine, and champagne).

Sometimes there is a requirement for a specific license if alcohol is to be served with food but not purchased separately. In still other instances a permit may be obtained when a cash bar will be provided, and still another permit when alcohol will be dispensed free.

The point is simple: Appropriate permits and licenses must be applied for and secured prior to the event where alcoholic beverages are served. Of course, the sponsoring organization may have other restrictions or prohibitions against serving alcohol, so check ahead of time to see.

If your organization serves alcohol, whether free or by means of a cash bar, it pays to be especially alert to a situation in which a patron becomes intoxicated. The negative consequences can be severe, both for the patron as well as for the individuals responsible for (and working at) the fund raising event and for the sponsoring organization. Sponsors and planners as well as servers at an event where a person consumes an excessive amount of alcohol are increasingly being held responsible for that person's actions.

No sport or recreation group wants to be involved in a DWI scandal, so those responsible for planning and implementing the fund raising project must take assertive action to prevent both underage drinking and overindulgence by those of legal age. Such actions could include, but not be limited to:

- Posting signs indicating that patrons will be asked for appropriate identification, and then carefully scrutinize the IDs.

- Making arrangements with a local cab company to drive home patrons who have overindulged in drink.

- Providing designated drivers from among the volunteers of the sponsoring group.

- Having experienced and skilled bartenders and servers of alcoholic beverages.

- Encouraging people at the event to team up with friends who are willing to be designated drivers.

- Not serving individuals under age or who already have consumed enough alcohol.

- Hiring off-duty police officers to help supervise the event.

These plans will help prevent negative consequences of excessive alcohol consumption and driving under the influence and will enhance the public's image of the sponsoring organization as sensible, caring, and proactive.

Sales

There are numerous fund raising projects that involve selling, and many direct sales efforts, especially door-to-door sales, involve youngsters as well as adult volunteers. Whenever young people are expected to sell door-to-door, they need to first receive appropriate safety instruction and sales training. Common safety rules instruct children to travel in pairs, be accompanied by an adult or older sibling, sell only within their own neighborhood unless accompanied by an adult, obey all traffic laws, and not venture out after dusk.

Instructing students and other volunteers how to sell successfully means teaching how to:

- identify safe environments in which to engage in selling

- identify and qualify potential customers

- approach them

- explain the product or service

- emphasize the benefit(s) to the purchaser(s)

- explain the nature of the non-profit sponsoring organization

- clarify how the money will benefit young people and sport or recreation programs

- handle objections, thank the prospect whether or not a purchase was made

- and maintain accurate records

Hard-sell or overaggressive tactics should be avoided. Remember, it is important that the prospective customer have a positive image of both the salesperson and the organization that the salesperson represents.

The time during which volunteers and staff are involved in the selling process is referred to as the selling window. In many instances, this selling window is kept to minimum amount of time, 3 to 4 weeks. Organizers want a concentrated amount of effort in a limited amount of time rather than to prolong the selling effort and risk losing enthusiasm and reducing the effectiveness of the sales force.

Adequate insurance coverage

Sometimes it is not possible to completely avoid all serious risks when involved in a fund raising project. To compensate for these risks fundraisers may choose to seek insurance coverage to protect those individuals who are involved in the fund raising project against lawsuits. Similarly, insurance coverage may be secured to protect against various types of loss associated with a fund raising effort. For example, an insurance policy can be secured to protect the organization against a contestant seeking to win a "million dollars" by hitting a hole in one on a golf course or sinking a full court basketball shot as part of a fund raising scheme. An insurance policy can also be secured to protect the organization and workers against lawsuits resulting from claims of negligence or carelessness.

Charging what the market will bear

One of the key questions facing everyone involved in fund raising is "how much should be charged" for the tickets, for the product, for the service, etc. The answer will vary in different communities and in different parts of the country. The fund raising principle states that organizers should charge "whatever the market will bear." The price of anything is dependent upon so many variables that the planners and organizers of the fund raising project will have to make that decision themselves in light of prevailing circumstances.

Sales tax

There are a variety of laws and regulations governing the collection of sales tax for fund raising activities by non-profit organizations. Whether it is necessary to collect sales tax when the sponsoring organization sells tickets, merchandise, or concession items is best left up to accountants or lawyers advising the fund raising organization. The key is to obtain, in writing, competent advice and counsel. Although the county tax collector or a representative of the state department of revenue will be able to answer many questions in this regard, many fundraisers play it safe by consulting a competent attorney or accountant in an effort to secure an expert opinion in this sometimes complicated area.

Permits, licenses, and permissions

There are many fund raising activities that involve door-to-door sales of items such as candy, tickets, chances, etc. Since many communities prohibit, restrict, or regulate door-to-door sales, it behooves fundraisers to comply fully with such requirements.

Some communities have implemented ordinances that restrict the activities of so-called transient retail merchants. A transient retail business is often thought of as a business conducted for less than 6 months; it can be located in the street, on the sidewalk, in front of or within a building, from a motor vehicle, or under a tent. Typically, the transient retail merchant ordinance is aimed at restricting or regulating flower vendors, magazine salespersons, car washers, and art merchants who display their merchandise and services at street intersections or in parking lots.

There are numerous examples of licensing fee exemptions for charitable organizations, groups from area school districts or colleges, recreation departments, city-sponsored organizations, and nationally recognized service organizations or clubs. Nevertheless, not all communities provide such blanket exemptions. As a result, it is prudent to check with the local municipal office that issues permits or licenses to see what requirements are applicable in your situation regarding hawking, peddling, and soliciting ordinance. Typically, the town clerk or bureau of licenses can issue such permits.

Another area where a permit is often required is when concession or food operations are involved in a fund raising project. In such an instance it is essential that you follow all health department regulations for food storage, preparation, and sale. And, you should secure all appropriate permits and licenses that regulate food and concession operations. Typically, these permits can be secured from the appropriate municipal offices within city hall or from the office of the town clerk.

Of course, securing permission and various permits and licenses is only part of the challenge. Equally important is adequately informing the staff, both paid and volunteers, about the regulations. It is imperative that they know what appropriate permits, licenses, and permissions require and allow. In the real world the licenses and permits that regulate food as well as door-to- door sales have many restrictions and covenants that must be strictly followed. Those responsible for the fund raising have the responsibility to see that the staff abide by the constraints of the licenses/permits.

Tools of the trade

Today, the tools of the trade for the modern fundraiser include not only the telephone but a fax machine, a computer, a quality printer and appropriate software (word processing, data base, presentation, graphics and desktop publishing). Some tools can be utilized to help reach potential donors and patrons. Other tools are used to create printed materials (programs, signs, flyers and posters) for the fund raising act itself. Of course, it is not necessary that those involved in fund raising actually purchase such tools. Rather, the volunteers and staff need only have access to them, preferably on a free basis, or at a greatly reduced cost. Additionally, access to the Internet, possession of an e-mail address and even a web page are quickly becoming necessities.

Record keeping

Accurate and timely record keeping is a hallmark of successful fund raising. Everyone involved must keep some kind of records: the organizers and planners of the fund raising projects, the young people and other volunteers, and even the booster clubs or athletic support groups. Some of the documentation that is often kept includes records of prospects, past donors, customers, alumni, inventory, vendors, budgets, income, expenses, pledges, items purchased for later sale, insurance, taxes, permits and licenses, minutes or summaries of meetings, copies of letters received and sent, and evaluations of past fund raising projects.

Nowhere is record keeping of greater importance than in the area of finance. Three key words where money is concerned: accuracy, accountability and security. Many schools, recreation departments and athletic programs require that all income from fund raising efforts be deposited in a special activity account. They also require that periodic reports of expenses and income (reconciliations and audits) be made to appropriate parties.

Additionally, all checks issued on such accounts usually require at least two (and sometimes three) signatures. Organizers need to pay special attention to financial record keeping; nothing can tarnish the reputation of a fund raising organization more effectively than mistakes or scandals associated with the handling of money.

Combining fund raising activities

A strategy that many promoters use to maximize fund raising profits is to combine activities. For example, the addition of a bake sale at a car bash site can increase the potential profit for the total experience. Another example is combining a formal sit-down dinner with a celebrity golf tournament. Thus, always be on the lookout for ways to increase profitability and enhance exposure by staging two or more activities at the same time and at the same site. This piggy-backing effort can be quite successful in generating increased interest, attendance and profit.

Scheduling fund raising activities

There are three kinds of fund raising activities in terms of timing. First, there is the fund raising project that can be conducted only once. For example, scheduling the *Souvenir Sport Paraphernalia Auction* or the *Donkey Basketball Competition* are examples of one-time fund raising events.

Second, there are fund raising efforts that lend themselves to being held each and every year, that is, to become an annual event. For example, the *Day*

Sport Camp. Every year there will be athletes as well as others who should be honored and recognized at a formal dining arrangement. The third type of fundraiser is one which can be repeated sometime in the future, but is not appropriate as an annual event. Examples might be the *Custom Bird House Auction,* the *Weight Loss Marathon,* or the *Great Duck Race.*

There are two significant advantages to implementing fund raising projects that can be repeated, either annually or periodically.

First, those who are involved in planning, organizing and implementing the fund raising project will have had experience with the project, thus making subsequent efforts much easier and more efficient and effective. Second, members of the general public who had attended or taken part in the fund raising activity in the past are more likely to repeat their involvement if the experience had been a positive one. Not only that, but through word of mouth a greater number of other individuals might know of the fund raising activity and be willing to become involved.

Don't forget to say "thanks"

An important concept of fund raising is to never forget to say "thanks" or provide public recognition to those individuals and organizations who helped you.

Not only is it common courtesy to do so, but such an effort also paves the way for continued help in the future. People like to be appreciated and thanked. They like to know that they have had a part in the success of the endeavor. Thus, take time and create opportunities to thank volunteers, helpers and those who have contributed in any way through donating money, goods or services to make your fund raising project a huge success. Doing so will reap big dividends in subsequent fund raising efforts.

Results of fund raising activities

Although obtaining actual cash is almost always the objective of any fund raising activity, organizers should never lose sight of the fact that sometimes goods and services are just as valuable. Goods or services that are contributed can be used to generate cash. For example, some donated goods (paintings, tickets, etc.) and services (free professional car washes), can be used in an auction to generate cold, hard cash. Or, other donated goods (computers, software, etc.) and services (free legal or accounting advice) can be used by the sponsoring organization in their day-to-day operation or in future fund raising activities. Thus, organizers need to think in terms of not only cash but also of services and goods which may enhance the overall operation of the sponsoring group.

There are many ways to accomplish the same objective

There are multiple ways to conduct any single fund raising project. In fact, 50 different organizations could devise 50 different ways to organize and implement one type of event—and each could be successful. Thus, it is up to you, the reader, to decide whether to use the projects outlined in this book "as is" or to adjust the ideas and adapt the concepts to suit your own unique circumstances.

After you have read this book, you should have a sound understanding of each of these fund raising projects. In addition, you should have a better concept of the basic elements of the fund raising process itself. With such knowledge, you should be able to use the ideas and tactics presented in this book to plan and implement any number of fund raising projects that can benefit your organization or program in terms of greater enthusiasm and support for your event, a more positive public image, and, most important, an increase in financial resources. I wish you much luck as you search for an appropriate and successful fund raising project.

Fund raising projects to generate up to $3,000

2

Chapter 2

Fund raising projects to generate up to $3,000

Fund raiser #1
Bake Sale(s)

POTENTIAL NET INCOME: $1,000 annually

COMPLEXITY/DEGREE OF DIFFICULTY: Low

DESCRIPTION: A bake sale consists of cookies, cakes, brownies, etc., being sold in a department or mall store. The bake sale "booth" consists of one or more card tables set up near the entrance to the store.

SCHEDULING: This fund raising project can be initiated at any time of the year. Holiday seasons are especially productive. The bake sale can scheduled periodically throughout the year at different stores or may be scheduled at a particular shop only during a particular weekend. Don't impose upon the generosity of the store or mall manager by attempting to set up a semi-permanent table almost every weekend. Instead, move to different stores in different malls or shopping centers throughout the year if the goal of the organization is to have an ongoing bake sale operation.

RESOURCES:

Facilities: Location is very important. Any store (Wal-Mart, Target, K-Mart, Ames, etc.) that enjoys heavy foot traffic is suitable. The more people that pass by the booth the greater the opportunity for sales and increased net profits. The space to erect the bake sale "booth" can be as small as 5' by 5'.

Equipment and supplies: Card tables, tablecloths, signs, change box, napkins and paper plates are all needed.

Publicity and promotion: Well designed, colorful posters and displays touting the availability of the delicious baked goods at the table(s) where the items are displayed comprise the guts of the publicity and promotional activities. Adults and youngsters staffing the "booth" should be most courteous in their solicitation of customers. If appropriate, have the youngsters dress in their sport uniforms. Additional photos and signs may be displayed outlining the type of activities sponsored by the sport or recreation organization. Be sure to highlight how the profits will be utilized.

Time: The baked goods can go on sale on a Saturday and Sunday from morning until late evening. Friday afternoons and evenings are also popular.

Expenditures: The costs for this project are minimal since all of the baked goods and related paper products are donated. Allocate $10 for the creation of signs and posters.

Personnel (Staff/Volunteers): Volunteers (5-15) are needed to donate baked goods as well as to help staff the "booth."

RISK MANAGEMENT: There is no financial risk involved since almost everything is donated. However, there is always a legal liability matter to be concerned with in terms of the quality of the baked goods. Be sure that you know who donates what items for the bake sale. Be hesitant to accept any donated food items from strangers. Also, require that all food be wrapped in plastic wrap, both for aesthetic and health purposes. Check with the sponsoring organization's insurance carrier to determine whether the organization and volunteers are covered in case of litigation regarding food poisoning, etc.

PERMITS/LICENSES: Check with the local health department, municipal bureau of licenses or the office of town clerk to see if a food permit or hawker's license is needed for the bake sale.

HINTS: Take advantage of the opportunity while selling the baked goods to also promote the organization itself, its volunteers and its many activities by displaying action photographs of the organization's pet projects and activities. Naturally, there should be a sign revealing how the profits from the sale will be used. Handouts publicizing the accomplishments and activities of the organization could also be given to customers and passersby. Some organizers also place a fish bowl on the table with a small sign requesting additional donations. In this bowl are placed several $1 and $5 bills to serve as a "hint" to prospective donors as to the type of donation being made. Some "booths" also sell coffee and/or cider.

Fund raiser #2
Pizza Extravaganza

POTENTIAL NET INCOME: $1,000

COMPLEXITY/DEGREE OF DIFFICULTY: Low

DESCRIPTION: The evening is billed as the community's GREATEST PIZZA EXTRAVAGANZA—admission free to the general public. The event itself is a pizza judging contest (conducted anonymously) with portions of all submitted pizzas sold to those in attendance at reasonable prices. Homemade and professionally prepared pizzas are judged in various categories and on various criteria, including but not limited to, taste, uniqueness of shape, variety of ingredients, decorations, etc. There may also be different age categories. Plus, there is an amateur and professional division. Donated prizes are awarded in each category. Each contestant is required to submit two identical, large-sized pizzas for each of the categories to be entered. Only one-third (4 slices) of one pizza is actually consumed by the judges. The remaining one and two-thirds (20 slices) of each submission are then sold to those present, during and following the judging process, for consumption on site or to take home. With fifty entrants in the various categories, there are 1000 slices of pizza available for sale at $1 a slice. Additional profit is from the sale of soft drinks.

SCHEDULING: This fund raising project can be scheduled as a stand-alone event or may be piggybacked with another activity of the sponsoring group. As a stand-alone event, the Pizza Extravaganza is held on a Friday or Saturday evening, from 7 p.m. to 9 p.m.

RESOURCES:

Facilities: An indoor site that will accommodate at least 100 individuals, with sufficient space for eating at tables, is required. Also, adequate and safe parking is a must.

Equipment and supplies: Display and eating tables; paper plates and napkins; plastic glasses, knives, and forks; soft drinks; garbage pails; rubber gloves (used by food handlers and judges); towels. Also, a microphone and sound system must be in working order. Posters, flyers and signs are needed for promotional purposes. Donated prizes are solicited from area merchants and organizations and could include trophies, ribbons, gift certificates and actual gifts. A cash box with $150 in change must be available at the site.

Publicity and promotion: Advertising and promotion for this fund raiser must emphasize its non-profit nature as well as the opportunity to partake of delicious and unusual pizzas created by both amateurs and professionals. Be sure to publicize how the money raised will be spent. Owners and managers of all local pizza shops in the area should be encouraged to take part by submitting their own pizzas in one or more categories. They can also serve as judges and promoters of the event. Signs, flyers and posters publicizing the free event and soliciting entrants for the pizza-making contest should be displayed in area businesses, especially the pizzerias.

Time: Planning for this fund raiser can be completed within two weeks. Promoting the contest should be limited to a 4-5 week window of opportunity. The actual judging and selling of the pizzas can be completed within a two-hour time period. Allow two hours for cleanup.

Expenditures: Less than $100 will be needed to get this project off the ground. Most of this money will be spent on promotion activities and securing soft drinks to resell during the evening. Most of the other supplies (eating utensils, etc.) can be secured by donations from businesses and/or supporters.

Personnel (Staff/Volunteers): Volunteers (5-7) and staff (1-2) will be needed to help promote and publicize the Pizza Extravaganza and to help out during the hours of the judging and the sale of pizza and soft drinks. Four hungry and impartial judges will also be needed. Finally, a popular master of ceremony will be successful in speeding along the activities of the evening while simultaneously serving as a source of entertainment and amusement.

RISK MANAGEMENT: Since all the pizza is donated, the financial risks are minimal. And, as long as proper health standards are observed, there should be no legal liability risks. However, doublecheck to insure that a fund raising activity such as the Pizza Extravaganza is included under the insurance coverage of the site where the event will be held.

PERMITS/LICENSES: A food or concession permit may be required. Check with the health department or town clerk to see if a special use permit is required.

HINTS: It is especially important to get the local pizzerias behind this fund raising event. Supporters of the fund raiser, who are also important and influential people within the community, should serve as the contact liaison with the managers/owners of these pizza shops to solicit their support and involvement.

Fund raiser #3
Thematic Commemorative Event and Dinner

POTENTIAL NET INCOME: $1,000

COMPLEXITY/DEGREE OF DIFFICULTY: Moderate

DESCRIPTION: This fund raiser revolves around a thematic commemorative event, such as (1) recognition of a coaching milestone, (2) remembrance of a special event or accomplishment, or (3) observance of an organization's anniversary–combined with an evening food gathering. In essence, commemorating the milestone, special event or anniversary are all excuses (but legitimate ones) to bring individuals together to break bread while generating sizeable income for the sport or recreation organization. Profit is generated from the sale of tickets to the dinner. The tickets are priced so that each one nets $10 profit for the sponsoring organization. Attendance depends upon the nature of the thematic event plus the effectiveness of the promotional and publicity efforts.

SCHEDULING: The dinner gathering is scheduled on a Friday or Saturday.

RESOURCES:

Facilities: A site suitable for hosting at least 100 for a formal sit-down dinner plus a separate area for cocktails is required. Safe parking is a must. A restaurant or party house is an ideal site although the cost will be considerably higher than if the dinner is held at its own facility. However, one difficulty in having a formal dinner at a facility other than a restaurant or party house is that the atmosphere is often lacking. Also, it is sometimes more difficult to adequately store, prepare and serve the food and drink to such a large number of patrons.

Equipment and supplies: If the dinner and commemorative festivities are being held at the sponsoring organization's own site, it is necessary to secure all the ordinary equipment and supplies required to put on a formal dinner. For example, a rectangular head table, 10-15 round tables each seating at least 10 guests, chairs, table decorations and lights, utensils, napkins, etc. A microphone and sound system must be available at the head table. Special plaques or certificates to be awarded to those individuals being honored or recognized must be secured.

Publicity and promotion: This special thematic, commemorative dinner event should be promoted on the basis of honoring individuals and/or remembering some past special event or achievement. However, don't neglect to highlight the non-profit nature of the sponsoring entity and how the money raised will be put to good use within the community. Signs and posters can be displayed throughout the area within various businesses and organizations. Ticket outlets can even be set up in some businesses. The area news media can be of significant assistance in publicizing the dinner event prior to and following the event.

Time: The thematic commemorative event can be planned and organized within a 2-week period. Promoting, advertising and selling advance tickets for the fund raiser can involve an additional 3-4 weeks. Allow 2 hours to get the facility set up for the gathering and another 2 hours for clean-up if the event is being held at the organization's own site. The length of a commemorative dinner will be approximately 90 minutes with an additional 20-30 minutes for the milestone, special event or anniversary.

Expenditures: Plan on spending $200 for promotional and publicity efforts. Allocate another $100 to cover the cost of certificates and/or plaques. The cost for the dinner will vary but plan on allocating $500 in initial seed money to reserve the site. Always attempt to reduce the expenses associated with the event by securing site rental, food and drinks, decorations, invitations, etc., on a free or reduced cost basis due to the non-profit nature of the sponsoring organization, the worthiness of the event itself, and the commendable purpose for which the profit will be spent.

Personnel (Staff/Volunteers): Volunteers (15-20) and staff (1-2) need to be actively involved in promoting and publicizing the commemorative event and in selling tickets. An additional 10-15 helpers are needed to put on the dinner if a restaurant is not chosen as the site. A popular and outstanding master of ceremony is an absolute must.

RISK MANAGEMENT: If alcohol is served, especially a cash bar, the organizers need to take steps to prevent excessive drinking and driving while under the influence. Those who might be in danger must be refused service. Also, providing designated drivers or free taxicab rides for people who may have over-indulged is a wise move in terms of reducing legal liability exposure and in terms of creating positive public relations.

PERMITS/LICENSES: There may be a need to secure a food and/or beverage permit or license if the event is held at the site of the sponsoring organization. Check with the local health department or town clerk.

HINTS: The more individuals being recognized or honored AND the more important or significant the milestone, event or anniversary—the greater the attendance. A cash bar will enhance net profits considerably.

Fund raiser #4
Singing Valentine

POTENTIAL NET INCOME: $1,100

COMPLEXITY/DEGREE OF DIFFICULTY: Low

DESCRIPTION: A singing group travels to a person's home or place of business and delivers a Valentine card, a carnation and sings two songs for Valentine's Day. The songs may include: (1) *My Funny Valentine,* (2) *Put Your Arms Around Me, Honey,* (3) *You Must Have Been A Beautiful Baby,* (4) *It Could Happen To You* (5) *I Can't Give You Anything But Love, Baby,* or (6) the perennial favorite, *Let Me Call You Sweetheart.* Of the $40 charged for each Singing Valentine, at least $25 reverts to the organizing group. The profits will be greater if the singing group donates its time and skill and if one or more corporate sponsors agree to underwrite any expenses associated with this fund raiser.

SCHEDULING: The delivery of the Singing Valentines should be scheduled for the weeks immediately preceding February 14. Naturally, most individuals or groups ordering the Singing Valentine will want the service on Valentine's Day. Since this is not always possible due to the large number of requests and the limited number of singing groups available, customers need to be convinced that delivery of the special "Valentines" on another day would be acceptable.

RESOURCES:

Facilities: The sponsors of this fund raiser will need to use an office or home where both phone and mail orders can be taken. If 50 reservations are made for the "Singing Valentines," the gross profit is $1,250.

Equipment and supplies: Valentine cards, carnations, posters, signs, markers, use of a free phone, receipt and record books and a cash box are all that are needed. The singers provide their own transportation. The cards, carnations and many other supplies should be obtained free of charge from local businesses or individuals. Or, at the very least, the supplies should be obtained at a greatly reduced cost because of the non-profit nature of this fund raising activity.

Publicity and promotion: Announcements of this service should appear in the local newspapers and penny-savers starting in early January. Local businesses and corporations should display signs or posters publicizing the Singing Valentines. The sponsoring organization should also utilize PA systems at other sporting or recreation events preceding February 14th. Be sure to publicize how the profits from this fund raising effort will be spent.

Time: The individual singing groups should be lined up by early December. The publicity surrounding this fund raiser should begin in early January and run continuously through Valentine's Day. Most of the requests for the Singing Valentine will be for the day itself and possibly the two weeks immediately preceding it.

Expenditures: This simplistic fund raising effort can be initiated for less than $100 in seed money. Ideally, the singers will donate their time and effort which will greatly increase the net profit.

Personnel (Staff/Volunteers): A small group of volunteers (2-4) and staff (1-2) is needed to plan and organize the project. Groups of singers (four or five different quartets) may be members of the booster or support group and/or may be chosen from local singing groups such as the Sweet Adeline's chorus or college fraternity or sorority glee club organizations.

RISK MANAGEMENT: There is little downside financial risk involved nor is there meaningful legal liability exposure due to the nature of the fund raising activity.

PERMITS/LICENSES: None.

HINTS: A variation of this fund raiser can be initiated at any time of the year under the title of "Singing Greetings." The sponsoring organization promotes the concept of a quartet of singers performing for any purpose (birthdays, engagements, births, anniversaries, "sweetest day," job promotions, etc.) on any specific date. Naturally, the visiting singers also provide a flower or two plus a suitably engraved card to a surprised recipient(s).

Fund raiser #5
Alumni(ae) Athletic Contests

POTENTIAL NET INCOME: $1,400

COMPLEXITY/DEGREE OF DIFFICULTY: Low.

DESCRIPTION: An athletic contest pitting alumni(ae) against current staff and/or volunteers is played before local fans and supporters. Profit is generated from admission fees ($3 or whatever the market will bear) plus concessions. If only 500 persons attend the event, the net profit, counting concessions, will approach $1,500.

SCHEDULING: The event is scheduled for a Friday evening, a Saturday afternoon or evening, or Sunday afternoon. The Alumni(ae) Athletic Contest can be a stand-alone event or can be piggy-backed with another activity or function of the sponsoring organization, either a fund raising activity such as a raffle, an auction or a non-fund raising function such as an open house, or dedication of a facility, etc.

RESOURCES:

Facilities: An appropriate competitive field or court is needed and dressing rooms for the competitors. Adequate parking must be available.

Equipment and supplies: Promoters need to provide athletic equipment and supplies necessary for the contest, including uniforms. A loud speaker system is advisable as is concession equipment, supplies and merchandise to sell. A first aid kit is highly recommended.

All such items should already be on hand for the sponsoring organization or able to be secured on a loan or no cost basis. Promotional signs, flyers and posters must be created.

Publicity and promotion: Mention of this special event should be included within all area news media, including the community penny-savers. Display of posters and signs within local businesses is highly recommended. Some of these businesses could also serve as ticket outlets. Tickets are available both on an advance basis and at the door. Promoters should approach local businesses in person in an effort to move advance tickets. Discounted group sales of tickets to businesses should be offered. Of course, supporters and members of the sponsoring entity should be approached as potential ticket purchasers.

Time: Planning for this fund raising can be as short as a week. However, gaining a firm commitment from the participants, both alumni(ae) and the local opposition, could involve several months. Similarly, scheduling the site for the competition should be done as early as possible, several months in advance at least. Promotional activities should begin some 5 weeks prior to the event with the actual ticket sale campaign taking place 3-4 weeks before. The actual contest can take up to 90 minutes. Cleanup will take less than an hour.

Expenditures: Anticipate spending less than $100 for publicity and promotional activities and materials.

Personnel (Staff/Volunteers): A highly dedicated group of volunteers (5-10) and staff (1-2) can plan and organize this event. These individuals can also serve as the core of the sales team for the marketing of the tickets for the Alumni(ae) Athletic Contest. An additional group of volunteers and staff (10-20) is needed to serve as the competition for the alumni group. Concessions and the ticket booth can be staffed by 5-8 motivated helpers. Of course, "impartial" volunteers are needed as officials for the contest. Inviting representatives of the medical profession is also highly recommended.

RISK MANAGEMENT: There is always the risk and danger of someone getting injured in this type of contest. Alumni(ae) and their opponents sometimes forget they are not as young and spry as they once were. As a result some individuals unfortunately tend to overexert themselves physically during such a contest. It is imperative that an athletic trainer, nurse or physician be in attendance in case someone is hurt. Having all competitors sign a Waiver of Responsibility for their participation is one method of protecting the sponsoring organization in terms of legal liability. The use of the waiver also reminds the participants that there is danger involved in any physical competition and that they should not participate with reckless abandon. There is little financial risk involved.

PERMITS/LICENSES: The only permit that might be needed is for the concession operation. All health codes must be adhered to in the operation of concessions. If the site of the competition is not owned by the sponsoring group, then formal permission must be obtained to reserve the facility.

HINTS: This can be a very easy fund raiser to plan and implement. Everyone involved should have an enjoyable time. It can also prove to be very beneficial in terms of positive publicity and public relations for all concerned. Following the competition there could be an opportunity for fans and those in attendance to mingle with the visiting alumni(ae). Depending upon the popularity of the guests and volunteers, an autograph session and/or photograph opportunity might be made available. If so, these should be mentioned in the publicity and promotional materials advertising the Alumni(ae) Athletic Contest.

Fund raiser #6
Playground Teen Dance

POTENTIAL NET INCOME: $1,500

COMPLEXITY/DEGREE OF DIFFICULTY: Moderate

DESCRIPTION: A recreation or sport organization sponsors a teen dance outside on a playground or a parking lot for youngsters in the community. Admission to this dance is limited to teenagers (high school students) within the local community or communities. Profit is generated through the sale of advance tickets ($5 per person or $7.50 per couple), sale of refreshments ($2,000 profit) and the solicitation of sponsors (10 sponsors paying $250 each) from the local businesses and organizations and from the Merchants Association. Only advance tickets are sold.

SCHEDULING: The dance can be scheduled on any Friday or Saturday evening when excellent weather is expected. In the event of inclement weather, a rain date is advertised well in advance.

RESOURCES:

Facilities: A large parking lot that could be roped off or otherwise isolated from non-participants would be an ideal location. Similarly, a street could be roped off and the dance held on the segregated street. The site needs to be capable of being "roped off" so that only those who purchased advance tickets would be able to take part in the official festivities.

Equipment and supplies: An excellent PA system for the band or disc jockey; tables and chairs; concession equipment and supplies (food, drink, candy, paper plates and cups, etc.); rope; signs, posters and flyers; tickets; trash containers and decorations are all required.

Publicity and promotion: The organizers should approach elected town officials as well as the area merchants association(s) and individual businesses to solicit their support as official sponsors of this teen dance. The support should be sought on the basis of two factors. First, youngsters in the area will be able to spend their time in a wholesome activity for that evening. Second, such financial assistance will enable the recreation or sport organization to use the profits from this dance for other worthwhile purposes within the community. Sponsorships in the amount of $200 are sought from individual businesses and organizations as well as from the merchant organization(s). Tickets are sold at all of the area high schools as well as through selected merchants. Signs and posters should be displayed throughout the community at businesses and organizations. Flyers can also be distributed on vehicles parked at malls and shopping centers. Of course, the local news media should play up this community event as part of their public service announcements.

Time: Planning and organizing this fund raiser will take several weeks. Securing the popular band may have to be done several months in advance. Setting up for the event will take 3-4 hours. The dance should start around 7:30 or 8 p.m. and conclude no later than 1 a.m. Plan on spending at least an hour to clean up the site.

Expenditures: Plan on spending up to $1,500 for a top band. Advertising and promotional efforts will cost another $250. A beginning concession inventory of $250 will be sufficient. If police presence is not donated, allocate another $250 for this assistance. It is worth it.

Personnel (Staff/Volunteers): To attract large numbers of youngsters to the dance it is imperative to hire a very popular band for the evening. An alternative is to hire a popular disc jockey who will play the top songs of the day. It is also very important that adult supervision (chaperones) be available and visible at all times. In some communities the authorities will assign police officers to the event as part of their regular duties that evening. In others, off-duty officers will have to be hired and paid (at $10-$12 an hour). Volunteers (20) and staff (2-3) will be needed to sell advance tickets and collect tickets at the door. Helpers will be needed to help publicize and promote the event. A cleanup committee is needed.

RISK MANAGEMENT: Adequate adult supervision reduces a great deal of the risk involved in this type of event. Financial risk is minimal because of the advance ticket sales and the solicitation of sponsors.

PERMITS/LICENSES: Check with the local town clerk and police authorities to see what type of permit is required to hold this event. A concession permit or license might also be required. Be sure to obtain permission to sell tickets at the local high schools, and to place flyers on windshields at area shopping centers and malls.

HINTS: There must be an absolute ban on all alcoholic beverages at this event. Also, implement the policy that once admitted to the dance, no one may leave and then re-enter. This prevents youngsters from sneaking out to "drink" and then returning to the dance. Be sure to provide sufficient trash containers. No tickets will be sold on the evening of the dance, thus eliminating last-minute gatecrashers or troublemakers. Selling advance tickets also helps in the planning for security, concession sales and cleanup activities. If this outdoor teen dance is a success, it can easily become an annual event, a very profitable one for the organizers and fun for the young people.

Fund raiser #7
"Take An Athlete to Dinner" Auction

POTENTIAL NET INCOME: $1,500

COMPLEXITY/DEGREE OF DIFFICULTY: Low

DESCRIPTION: Individual athletes, recreation personnel, coaches and/or administrators, and others are "auctioned off" on an individual basis to the highest bidders. There is a minimum beginning bid of $25. Typically, the average amount bid for each will be in the $50 range. If 30 individuals are to be "auctioned," the profit approximates $1,500. Each winning bidder selects the site for dinner, which takes place within the following three weeks.

SCHEDULING: The auction may be scheduled at any time of the year, and may be held in conjunction with a sporting event or recreation activity or as a stand-alone event.

RESOURCES:

Facilities: Any site which can accommodate a large number of bidders may be used. A gymnasium, a classroom, a dining facility, etc., can all be appropriate sites.

Equipment and supplies: A PA system, cash box, record book, tables and chairs are necessary. Additionally, signs and posters for publicity.

Publicity and promotion: Advance publicity for the auction should include mention in area newspapers, including penny-savers. Announcements should also be made at other events sponsored by the organizing group as well as other community groups. Area businesses can be asked to display signs and posters. Highlight the non-profit nature of this fund raising effort as well as how the profit is to be used.

Time: This simple fund raising project can be planned and organized within a week. Signing up the individuals to be "auctioned" off can take up to 10 days. The publicity campaign should be limited to 3-4 weeks. The auction itself can be completed within an hour or two, depending upon the number of individuals involved.

Expenditures: This fund raising event can be run for less than $100.

Personnel (Staff/Volunteers): A master of ceremony is needed to act as the auctioneer to lend an atmosphere of authenticity. Many auctioneers will donate their services and expertise if the auction is for a non-profit purpose. Additional volunteers (7-10) and staff (1-2) are needed to help with advance publicity and promotional activities as well as to help run the "auction."

RISK MANAGEMENT: There is little financial risk involved. Similarly, the legal liability exposure is minimal. The worst that could happen is that an individual might not even receive the minimum bid, which in itself could be quite embarrassing both for the individual and for the sponsoring organization. To prevent this catastrophe from occurring, organizers need to prearrange with "ringers" in the audience to bid the minimum amount (and be willing to take the individual to dinner) if there are no other bids.

PERMITS/LICENSES: If the "auction" is of school athletes, doublecheck with the appropriate conference, state and/or national governing bodies to insure that no rules or regulations are violated by taking athletes out to dinner. No organizing group would want to be involved in an embarrassing situation in which the athletes' eligibility is inadvertently placed in jeopardy as a result of this fund raising project.

HINTS: Be sure the individuals who are "auctioned off" write personal "thank-you" letters to each of their successful bidders expressing appreciation for their financial contributions and a wonderful dining experience.

Fund raiser #8
All You Can Eat Ziti Feast

POTENTIAL NET INCOME: $2,000

COMPLEXITY/DEGREE OF DIFFICULTY: Moderate

DESCRIPTION: A buffet dinner is held featuring ziti and cheese sauce, garlic bread, green salad, iced tea, coffee and lemonade. Donated homemade desserts may also be made available. The prices of the dinner tickets are set to enable the sport or recreation organization to realize a profit of approximately

$4 for every adult ticket sold and $2 for every children's ticket. Tickets are sold in advance and at the door. With 500 individuals taking part the net profit can easily approach $2,000.

SCHEDULING: The feast can be scheduled on any Saturday, from 11 a.m. to 8:30 p.m. Or, organizers may choose instead to schedule the ziti feast on two consecutive evenings, Friday and Saturday, from 3:30 p.m. to 8:30 p.m. each day.

RESOURCES:

Facilities: A site with cooking facilities, capable of seating 100 - 150 or more at a single sitting, is needed. Adequate parking is an absolute must. It is a significant advantage if the site is on or near a heavily traveled roadway so as to attract many people who happen to drive or walk by.

Equipment and supplies: All of the paraphernalia necessary to store, prepare, cook and serve the various food items must be available. Similarly, tables and chairs must be on hand for the patrons to sit down and dine. Tablecloths, napkins, plastic cutlery, paper plates and cups, and table and room decorations are all necessary. Signs, flyers and posters must be created for publicity purposes. Don't forget tickets, receipt books and cash boxes.

Publicity and promotion: The ziti dinner is promoted as a non-profit fund raising project sponsored by a local charitable, service, educational or sport organization. Be sure to include how the profits will be spent within the community in the promotions and publicity. The dinner needs to be publicized through the local news media, including the penny-savers. Local businesses can play a big part by displaying signs, flyers and posters. The sponsoring group can also utilize its own PA system(s) at other events (athletic contests or recreational activities) that it conducts in advance of the date of the dinner. A large outdoor sign should be erected outside the site to attract potential patrons.

Time: The planning and organizing of this fund raiser can take up to 2 weeks. It may take 3-4 weeks, however, to line up all the helpers and the donations needed for this event to be a truly successful affair. Allow 3-4 weeks of intensive promotion and advertising. Preparation and set-up on the day of the event will take 3-4 hours. Cleanup can easily take 3 hours if done properly.

Expenditures: The organizers should also attempt to secure as many items as possible on a donated or loan basis. This is especially true in terms of the food items, decorations, usage of the dining facility, cooking equipment and serving utensils. Ideally, the sponsoring organization will use its own facility or another site at no cost or for a truly nominal fee. Allocate $150 for promotional and publicity efforts, including advertisements in media and creation of signs, flyers and posters. Be sure to have sufficient change on hand, at least $150.

Personnel (Staff/Volunteers): People are the real key to this fund raising project. Volunteers (30-35) and staff (2-4) are needed to help in promoting and advertising efforts, to sell advance tickets and tickets at the door, to prepare and serve the food, to help set up the facility, to periodically clean the tables as well as to assist in cleaning up after the last patron is served.

RISK MANAGEMENT: The financial risks are greatly reduced if the use of the site is free or relatively inexpensive and if most of the food and drink items are donated. Selling advance tickets is another way to diminish the risk of preparing too much food for the number of paying patrons. To reduce or eliminate legal liability exposure, all health rules and regulations pertaining to the handling of food must be strictly observed. Check to insure that the site's blanket insurance policy adequately covers the sponsors and the owner(s) for this type of event.

PERMITS/LICENSES: A special food permit might be required for this fund raiser. Check with the health department or town clerk.

HINTS: Not all of the food need be prepared at the site of the dinner. However, if this is the case, then the items that are prepared elsewhere must be transported to the facility where the dinner is held. It is imperative to secure donated food and drink items as well as having sufficient volunteers willing to donate their time, services and expertise in the preparation, cooking and serving of the food. Additional profits may be realized if take-out orders are made available and publicized in advance.

Fund raiser #9
Stay-At-Home (Pseudo) Extravaganza

POTENTIAL NET INCOME: $2,000

COMPLEXITY/DEGREE OF DIFFICULTY: Low

DESCRIPTION: Potential contributors are solicited to donate what they would have spent (or a portion thereof) on actual tickets, transportation, meals, baby-sitting services, etc., to one or more nationally or locally televised sporting and/or non-sporting events while, in fact, staying home and watching the actual event on television. A mechanism by which the donors may sign up for this fund raiser and pledge their donation(s) is provided in the form of a card and a self-addressed envelope. If 75 individuals contribute an average of $30 towards this event, the promoters have earned a gross profit of $2,250. If 100 individuals end up contributing only $15 the gross profit is a sizeable $3,000 for a minimum of effort.

SCHEDULING: This fund raising tactic can be scheduled around a single event on a specific date (state high school basketball championship(s),

Macy's Holiday Parade, a theatre event, the NCAA, division I basketball championship, the Super Bowl, etc.). Thus, the invitations and promotional activity can be centered around that specific event. Another possibility is to involve any number of events taking place at different times throughout the upcoming months. In that eventuality the invitations can mention a number of special events on different dates and encourage would-be contributors to pick one or more of these activities on which to base their contribution(s).

RESOURCES:

Facilities: A room is needed to prepare and mail out envelopes.

Equipment and supplies: Invitations, cards, envelopes and stamps are needed to mail out to the prospect pool. Posters, flyers and information sheets are also needed for marketing and promotional purposes. And a self-addressed return envelope will be needed to facilitate mailing in contributions.

Publicity and promotion: The most effective promotional activities involve individual person-to-person contacts. However, mailings to individuals and businesses who are predisposed to supporting sports and/or recreational activities in the community should not be overlooked. A suitably engraved and clearly stated invitation aimed at prospective donors is a must. Such an invitation can be used both in the mail campaign and in the person-to-person contacts. Promoters find that a flyer or printed handout concisely detailing exactly how the Stay-At-Home Extravaganza works is invaluable in "selling" the concept. All of the promotional efforts should outline the purpose(s) of this fund raising effort and specifically highlight how the money will be put to good use. Don't forget to promote this fund raising event over the public address system at other activities or competitions of the sponsoring organization.

Time: The planning phase of this fund raiser can be completed within a week or two. The actual implementation will take longer. The most time-consuming activities are the marketing, publicizing and actual selling of the idea to prospective donors. Keep this so-called selling window short, no longer than 4 weeks.

Expenditures: Minimal expenditures are needed. Creation of formal invitations, self-addressed envelopes, attractive flyers and posters displayed within community businesses, as well as informational sheets, are the major expenditures, less than $150. Stamps and envelopes will total less than $100.

Personnel (Staff/Volunteers): A group of 20-25 volunteers supported by one or two professional staff can be most effective in selling this concept to a significant portion of qualified prospects in the community.

RISK MANAGEMENT: There is always risk in this type of fund raising activity that potential prospects will not readily understand what this so-called EXTRAVAGANZA really is all about and how it operates. That is why a well trained group of salespeople is vital for effective person-to-person contacts. Similarly, the information flyer to accompany the invitations sent in the mail must be crystal clear in terms of explaining the fund raiser. There is minimal financial risk ($250) and legal liability is almost non-existent.

PERMITS/LICENSES: None.

HINTS: An effective marketing approach with this fund raiser is to provide a list of 10-25 upcoming events which will be televised in the upcoming months and asking which of the events they would like to be able to see in person if given the chance. From that beginning, the prospects are then introduced to the concept that they can see the same event on television and can put the money which would have been spent to productive use for a good cause by contributing to the sport or recreation program. The success of this entire scenario rests in convincing would-be donors of the value of the sport or recreation program(s).

Fund raiser #10
Cheerleading Competition

POTENTIAL NET INCOME: $2,100

COMPLEXITY/DEGREE OF DIFFICULTY: Moderate

DESCRIPTION: Cheerleading teams representing area junior and senior high schools are invited to participate in a competition. Donated prizes are awarded to both team and individual winners in various categories. Profit is generated from an entry fee charged each team, an admission charge to view the competition and the sale of concession items. The entry fee can range from $25 to $75, or whatever the market will bear in your area. The gross profit is $1,400 if only 40 cheerleading squads enter the competition with each paying a $35 entry fee. Add to this figure $500 profit from the concession stand and $750 as a result of admission fees and the gross profit comes to $2,650. A free cheerleading clinic or workshop is conducted for all of the competitors and their parents prior to the start of the actual competition. A videotape is made of the entire competition and duplicates are then sent to each of the cheerleading squads with a personal "thank-you" letter some weeks after the competition.

SCHEDULING: The competition can be scheduled on a Saturday or Sunday during the months of September through January. Be sure to doublecheck so that the competition is not scheduled when the cheerleading squads will be busy cheering their respective teams.

RESOURCES:

Facilities: A gymnasium or large auditorium will suffice. There must be sufficient room for the cheerleading squads to perform their routines and also adequate seating for spectators. Adequate and safe parking should be close by.

Equipment and supplies: Donated prizes (trophies, ribbons, certificates), signs, posters, PA system, tables, chairs, blank video tapes, stationary, stamps as well as concession equipment and supplies must be available. The use of a computer and laser printer is also necessary in order to send out personal letters or invitations. A video camera can be borrowed to tape the competition. Additionally, borrowed VCRs are required to make duplicates (to be mailed to each school) of the original tape.

Publicity and promotion: Individual letters must be sent to cheerleading advisers at all area schools. Personal phone calls should also be made. Announcements in the media and the display of signs and posters by local businesses and organizations will help publicize the fund raiser.

Time: This fund raising event can be planned and organized within a week. It may take 5-6 weeks to send out invitations and to secure commitments from the various schools. Be sure to reserve well in advance the facility where the competition is to be held. The cheerleading clinic will last 90 to 120 minutes, between 9 a.m. and 11 a.m. The competition will begin at 12:30 or 1 p.m. and continue into the late afternoon or early evening, depending on the number of teams.

Expenditures: Allocate $200 to pay for the expert to conduct the clinic. Another $150 will be spent for promotional and publicity efforts. Allocate $200 if the videotapes and prizes (ribbons, certificates and/or trophies) are not donated.

Personnel (Staff/Volunteers): A cheerleading expert (contact a nearby university) should conduct the clinic. Volunteers (4-5) are needed to serve as judges. The concession stand can be staffed by 10-15 helpers working staggered hours. An announcer or master of ceremonies is also needed as is a certified trainer (in case of injuries). Altogether, 15-25 volunteers are needed.

RISK MANAGEMENT: There is minimal financial risk due to the fact that reservations are confirmed and the entry fees are received prior to the date of the competition. However, there is always a danger of physical injury whenever sophisticated cheerleading stunts are performed. Thus, to reduce the likelihood of injuries (as well as the prospects of successful lawsuits) it is necessary to place restrictions on the type of stunts used. Obviously dangerous stunts, such as three-level pyramids, should be prohibited. Require spotters for all elevated routines.

PERMITS/LICENSES: It may be necessary to obtain a concession permit in order to sell food and drink at the site. Check with the health department or town clerk in your community.

HINTS: The early morning workshop or clinic is a very important part of the day's activities. Some organizers bring in collegiate cheerleaders or cheerleading squads as well as their coaches so that these experienced performers might demonstrate advanced skills as well as emphasize the basics involved in cheerleading. The fact that the morning workshop is separated from the actual competition by 60 to 90 minutes gives the organizers an almost captive audience, competitors and their parents and friends, who will most likely purchase lunch on the premises. This fund raising event can easily become an annual affair which everyone anticipates.

Fund raiser #11
"Art in All Media" Auction

POTENTIAL NET INCOME: $2,500

COMPLEXITY/DEGREE OF DIFFICULTY: Low

DESCRIPTION: An art auction (billed as "Art in All Media") sponsored by a sport or recreation group takes place on a single evening. A gallery or professional art dealer provides paintings, posters and numbered prints of unknown as well as well-known artists (Alaniz, Agam, Calder, Delacroix, Rockwell, Moses, Bonlanger, Lubeck, Chagall). Additionally, a variety of popular sport art and posters are also available. One such art gallery is Marlin Art Inc., 920 Grand Blvd., Deer Park, New York 11729 (516-242-3344). The profit to the sponsoring organization is generated either by taking a flat $1,000 payment from the art dealer (if there are at least 150 people in attendance at the auction) or receiving 10% of the gross amount bid for the various art pieces. Additional profits are created from a bake sale and other refreshments that are sold during the evening's auction.

SCHEDULING: The art auction can be scheduled for any Friday or Saturday evening. Good weather is conducive to a larger turnout of prospective bidders.

RESOURCES:

Facilities: An indoor site that can hold approximately 250-400 prospective bidders is suggested. There must be room to display all of the art pieces as well as a place to set up a refreshment stand. There must be adequate safe parking.

Equipment and supplies: A quality microphone and speaker system for the auctioneer must be made available. Posters, signs and special invitations should be created to help publicize and promote the event. Stamps and envelopes will be needed to mail the invitations. Chairs and tables should also be set up for the auction. All auction paraphernalia is provided by the art gallery.

Publicity and promotion: All of the fans, boosters and members of the organizing group as well as the general public should be encouraged to attend by means of announcements at other community events. Newspapers (including penny-savers) should also carry information about the upcoming art auction. Even radio and television stations might be willing to include a blurb about the auction as part of their public service announcements. Ask local businesses and organizations to display signs highlighting the auction. Be sure to promote the fact that this is a fund raising project sponsored by a non-profit group. Also, publicize how the anticipated profits will be used within the community. Send special invitations to interior decorators in your area since these individuals are always on the outlook for interesting paints, prints and posters.

Time: This project can be planned and organized within a week. The publicity and promotional activities should take up no more than 3-4 weeks. The event begins at 7 p.m. with an opportunity for the visitors to preview the pieces to be auctioned. At 8 p.m. the auction officially begins and concludes around 10:30 p.m.

Expenditures: The only costs involved in this fund raising project might be $50 for publicity and promotional efforts. Ideally, however, the signs, posters, invitations and refreshments are obtained on a donated (or at least greatly reduced price) basis. Even postage can be donated by having individual boosters or local businesses mail invitations. Naturally, the site is available on a donated basis.

Personnel (Staff/Volunteers): A limited number of volunteers (10-15) and staff (1-2) is needed to make this event a success. For example, helpers are needed to plan and organize this event. This involves reserving the site, confirming arrangements with the gallery, helping out with the promotional and publicity campaign, setting up and staffing the refreshment/concession stand, and cleaning up after the event. The gallery or art dealer provides an experienced, professional art auctioneer and accompanying support staff (hawkers, ring personnel, bookkeepers).

RISK MANAGEMENT: There are few financial risks associated with this fund raiser. If the sponsors are conservative they might choose the $1,000 profit guaranteed if there are at least 150 people in attendance. For the more adventuresome, the sponsors can gamble on receiving 10% of the amount bid for the prints. The liability exposure is greatly reduced, if not eliminated, if health rules and regulations are strictly adhered to in connection with the refreshments. Be sure to deal with a reputable art dealer/gallery. You want to rest assured that the items to be auctioned are of acceptable quality. You want the bidders to be satisfied with their purchases so that this might become an annual or biannual event.

PERMITS/LICENSES: A permit might be necessary for the concession or refreshment stand. Check with the local town clerk or bureau of licensing. HINTS: This fund raiser is truly a turnkey project in that most of the work is done by the art gallery or dealer. There should be no problem in getting at least 150 people in the audience, especially if fans and boosters of the sponsoring group will support the event. If the publicity and promotional campaign is effective there should be a very large group in attendance with the potential for a significant gross bid amount.

Fund raiser #12
Breakfast with the Easter Bunny

POTENTIAL NET INCOME: $2,500

COMPLEXITY/DEGREE OF DIFFICULTY: Moderate

DESCRIPTION: Little children (and their parents) are invited to take part in a gathering (lasting approximately 45 minutes) with the Easter Bunny at which time breakfast (orange juice, milk and donuts) is provided for the youngsters. An individual Polaroid picture is taken of each child with the Easter Bunny. Small gift packages containing safety suckers, jellybeans, and coloring sheets are provided for each child. Non-competitive games and other activities appropriate to the individual children's ages are also provided. Profit is realized by charging $10 per child. Tickets are available at the door as well as through advance sales. With only 300 youngsters involved the profit approaches a very respectable $2,500.

SCHEDULING: This fund raising project consists of several different Saturday or Sunday mornings preceding Easter when children are able to enjoy breakfast with the Easter Bunny.

RESOURCES:

Facilities: Any large, clean room such as a gymnasium would be sufficient to host this event. Ideally, the site should be close to heavily traveled foot and vehicular traffic so as to attract a large number of drive-by patrons. Adequate parking facilities must be available close to the site.

Equipment and supplies: A Polaroid camera, film, tickets, tables, chairs, paper napkins, cups and plates, orange juice, milk and donuts as well as gift packages containing safety suckers, jelly beans, and coloring sheets must be secured, hopefully on a donated (or reduced cost) basis. Signs and posters need to be created for publicity purposes. A tarp should be available to place over the floor where the youngsters will eat. And, of course, an Easter Bunny costume is an absolute must.

Publicity and promotion: It is essential that publicity be disseminated throughout the community well in advance. Announcements should appear in the local papers and might be included in the public service announcements of the area radio and television stations. To increase the visibility of the event, there should be a large, easily seen, sign or poster outside the site where the breakfast is to be held. Area businesses should display signs and posters. Advance tickets can also be sold by select businesses. The sponsors should utilize the PA system at other community events to publicize and promote the upcoming breakfast.

Time: The project can be planned and organized within a week's time. Advance publicity efforts and ticket selling can take 4-5 weeks. The event officially opens at 9 a.m. and will close at 11:30 a.m. Within this time frame there can be three different groups of youngsters taking part. The first group begins at 9 a.m. and concludes at 9:45 a.m. The second group begins at 10:00 a.m. and ends at 10:45 a.m. The third and last group of children that day begins at 11:00 a.m. and will leave at 11:45 a.m. Each time segment will be filled with a variety of non-competitive games and activities followed by photographs with the Easter Bunny and then breakfast.

Expenditures: Rental of a superb bunny costume will cost up to $75. Don't skimp on the costume. Refreshments (food and drink) and small gift packages for the breakfasts should be donated. If not, plan on spending $400 for food and trinkets. Allocate $100 for publicity efforts.

Personnel (Staff/Volunteers): Volunteers (25-30) are the foundation of this fund raising project. An uninhibited individual should assume the role of the Easter Bunny. A skilled photographer is needed. Additional helpers are needed to pick up and distribute the food and drink, to organize the games and activities for the children and to collect the money and pre-sold tickets at the door. Volunteers should be organized into teams to sell the tickets within the community. Both person-to-person contacts as well as phone contacts should be used in marketing the tickets. Finally, don't forget about the clean-up committee.

RISK MANAGEMENT: If the event is held in a gymnasium (with wood floors) be sure to place a tarp over the floor where the children will be drinking and eating. The financial risks are diminished if sufficient advance tickets are sold within the community. Legal liability exposure is held to a minimum if all regulations and rules pertaining to food and drink are strictly followed and if adequate adult supervision is present.

PERMITS/LICENSES: As long as there is no actual food preparation (cooking) involved there is usually no need for any type of food license or permit. However, to play it safe, you can contact the health department or the office of the town clerk.

HINTS: College students majoring in physical education or recreation or elementary education are ideal volunteers to help your organization in terms of organizing appropriate games and other non-competitive activities for the little ones.

Fund raiser #13
Boat and RV Show

POTENTIAL NET INCOME: $2,500

COMPLEXITY/DEGREE OF DIFFICULTY: Low

DESCRIPTION: A free boat and recreational vehicle (RV) show is held on the property owned by the sport or recreation organization. The profit is obtained from a $250 fee (or, whatever the market will bear) charged to each exhibiting boat and RV dealer. A concession stand creates an additional profit center.

SCHEDULING: The show starts at noon on Friday and runs through the weekend, concluding at 5 p.m. on Sunday. The outdoor event is held in the early spring. Advertise an alternative rain date for severe inclement weather.

RESOURCES:

Facilities: An outdoor site suitable for displaying both boats and recreational vehicles. Ample and secure parking is also necessary for those visiting the show. The facility should be near a high traffic area.

Equipment and supplies: Posters, signs and flyers should be distributed throughout the community and displayed by area businesses. Portable water coolers and restrooms ("port-a-pots") will need to be provided if none are at the site. Although some signage will be provided by individual vendors there will be a need for a general sign on site publicizing the event. A cash box, record book, money bags and inventory are needed for the concession operation. First aid equipment and supplies should be on hand in case of illness or accident.

Publicity and promotion: The publicity for the event centers around advertisements placed 3-4 weeks prior to the date of the show and continuing right up until Saturday morning of the weekend of the show. Flyers or signs, some posted on telephone poles, should be strategically located near the site to help direct traffic to the Boat and RV Show. Pro bono announcements by area news media are extremely helpful in getting the message out to the public. Individual boat and RV vendors will place their own advertisements in the media in an attempt to attract their own clientele to the show and to their vehicles.

Time: Three to four months advance planning is necessary to line up the boat and RV dealers, secure the site location and to work out the marketing strategy and advertisement plan of action. Plan on 4-5 hours for the dealers to actually move their vehicles to the site to prearranged display areas. Another 4-5 hours will be needed to remove the boats and RVs from the site.

Expenditures: Less than $200 in expenses need be incurred for advertising and signage. First aid supplies can be obtained on a donated basis. Plan on spending another $100 for concession items to be resold.

Personnel (Staff/Volunteers): Volunteers and staff (5-10) are needed to canvas the area boat and RV dealers to sell them upon the idea of participating in the show. These spokespersons for the fund raising organizations should be centers of influence ("heavy hitters") and be skilled and convincing if the event is to attract a sufficient number of important vendors. Additional staff (1-2) and volunteers (5-10) are needed to help publicize and promote the free event to the general public. And, the concession stand needs to be continually staffed by a group of 3-5 people, working in 4-hour shifts. This could involve another 35 volunteers.

RISK MANAGEMENT: Be sure that all vendors understand any restrictions or limitations that are placed upon them prior to their arrival on site. For example, dealers might be limited to a maximum number of boats and RVs depending upon the available space. Also, the exact location of each dealer's inventory must be stipulated well in advance so that there is no misunderstanding on the day of the event. There always seems to be a logistical challenge when ten or more dealers and vendors bring a total of 100 or more RVs and boats to a single site. There is minimal financial risk involved for the sponsoring organization since commitments and entrance fees ($250) are secured prior to the event. Legal liability exposure is kept to a minimum through the blanket coverage of the insurance policy held by the owners of the site. But be sure to check out the policy.

PERMITS/LICENSES: Check with the city and county municipal offices for possible permits that may be required for this type of event. However, if the site is owned by the sport or recreation department there may be no special permits necessary, although a concession permit might be necessary. Check with the local municipal offices such as the town clerk. Be sure to follow all health department rules and regulations pertaining to the preparation, storage and sale of food and drink.

HINTS: Allocation of space can be determined on a "first committed-first served" basis. That is, those dealers who commit and pay the exhibit fee first will get priority in choosing among the available display areas. Once this type of show is successful, subsequent shows will be able to be organized with less effort and with likelihood of increased attendance—by both boat and RV dealers and the public.

Fund raiser #14
Hands-On Marathon

POTENTIAL NET INCOME: $2,500

COMPLEXITY/DEGREE OF DIFFICULTY: Moderate

DESCRIPTION: Fifty final contestants are chosen by chance to participate in a hands-on marathon which involves continually touching (with a single hand) the big prize, such as a large screen television set, a stereo system or even a vehicle. The moment each contestant fails to maintain constant physical contact with the prize that individual is eliminated from the contest. The last person left touching the prize wins. To be eligible to be one of the final 50 contestants, one must purchase a ticket and have that ticket drawn at a prior drawing. Each ticket sells for $5, or three for $10.

SCHEDULING: The hands-on marathon should be kicked off on a Friday afternoon and continues uninterrupted until there is only one remaining person touching the grand prize. The selection of the 50 contestants is completed a week before at a prior sporting or recreation event. At that time all tickets sold are placed in a drum or large fish bowl and the 50 participants are drawn. This provides an opportunity for the 50 finalists to have a week to prepare for their involvement in the marathon.

RESOURCES:

Facilities: An indoor site that is open to the public is needed. For example, the center aisle in a shopping mall or within a large discount store is ideal. What is needed is a public place that attracts a large amount of foot traffic and is able to be roped off, thus allowing the contestants to be visible, but yet undisturbed, in their efforts to continue touching the big prize. The site owners must allow the hands-on marathon to continue unabated when the store is closed to the public.

Equipment and supplies: Securing the grand prize—whatever that happens to be—is the first order of business. Some organizers give away a car. Others give a large television set. Still others award a free vacation trip (in which case the contestants attempt to continue to touch a portable wall or display erected for that purpose). Naturally, the greater the value of the prize the more money must be raised and more tickets sold. Signs, posters, tickets, ropes, stanchions, a large fish bowl or drum, tables and chairs are also necessary.

Publicity and promotion: Extensive publicity within the community and surrounding areas is essential. Promote the non-profit nature of the fund raiser and how the money will be put to use. Signs and posters promoting the marathon and illustrating the grand prize must also be displayed in area businesses, some of which may also serve as ticket outlets. News media should carry timely announcements. The store or mall manager can help in promoting the event by displaying the grand prize, with suitable signage, in a conspicuous place for all to see, during 3-4 weeks prior to the start of the marathon. Also, by making periodic announcements over the PA system. The site should also provide a viewing area with chairs for the general public. Announcements should also be made and tickets sold at other events of the sponsoring organization prior to the marathon.

Time: This fund raiser can be planned and organized within a two-week period. However, allow 4-6 weeks to secure a suitable grand prize or prizes. The official introduction of the hands-on marathon is not made until the grand prize is secured. After the announcement, plan on spending 3-4 weeks on promotional efforts and concentrated ticket selling. Allow several hours to set up the site. The hands-on marathon starts at 3 p.m. on a Friday and continues uninterrupted until there is only one contestant remaining who is touching the big prize.

Expenditures: The grand prize to be given away is potentially the greatest expense involved in this fund raiser. However, the organizers should attempt to secure this prize on a free (donated) basis or, at the very least, at a greatly reduced cost.

Personnel (Staff/Volunteers): Volunteers (5) and staff (1-2), who are important centers of influence within the business community, are needed to solicit a donation of a suitable grand prize. Other helpers (10-15) are needed to take part in the promotional and publicity efforts, to sell tickets and to serve as judges, on a rotating basis.

RISK MANAGEMENT: The financial risk is minimized if the grand prize is secured before the fund raiser is officially announced and tickets are sold. Check with the manager of the store or mall to insure that this type of fund raising event is covered under the site's umbrella insurance policy.

PERMITS/LICENSES: Since the drawing is a form of gambling, check with the local authorities to determine whether a special permit or license is required. HINTS: Some promoters have found success in giving away more than just the so-called big prize. In these instances, other highly desirable prizes, are awarded to the 2nd, 3rd, 4th, 5th, and so on, winners in the hands-on marathon. When people have more chances of winning an item(s) of true value, the more attractive the contest becomes—and more tickets are sold.

Fund raiser #15
Square Dance Round-Up

POTENTIAL NET INCOME: $2,500

COMPLEXITY/DEGREE OF DIFFICULTY: Moderate

DESCRIPTION: A fun-filled evening of square dancing is planned for both novices and experienced dancers. The dance party is advertised as an Open House or Round-Up in which participants of different skill levels are able to enjoy themselves to the fullest. Lessons are available for both the beginning and intermediate levels. Advance dance demonstrations are also provided by members of a local square-dance organization. Advance tickets are $25 per couple and $30 at the door. Refreshments are sold throughout the event at a concession stand operated by the organizing group.

SCHEDULING: The dance party is held on any Friday or Saturday evening. Any time of the year is suitable for a Square Dance Round-Up.

RESOURCES:

Facilities: A site that can accommodate between 100-150 couples is required. Adequate parking should be available adjacent to the site.

Equipment and supplies: Refreshments, signs, posters, flyers, markers, tables, chairs, decorations and door prizes are all necessary. Most, if not all, of these items can be secured on a donated or greatly reduced cost from local businesses and organizations.

Publicity and promotion: Promotional and publicity efforts should emphasize the availability of group square-dance instruction for people of all ages as well as opportunities for more experienced dancers to do their thing. Advertisements in area newspapers and penny-savers are a must. Similarly, local radio and television stations can include mention of this unique fund raising effort through their Public Service Announcements (PSAs). Local businesses can display signs or posters promoting the upcoming dance and some organizations can even serve as advance ticket sites. Businesses that cater to the square-dancing crowd should be sought as corporate sponsors in exchange for money as well as door prizes. These businesses can also purchase block tickets to give away as part of their in-store promotions. Flyers should be placed on vehicles parked at area malls and shopping centers.

Time: This fund raiser can be conceptualized within a week. Reserve the facility at least 4-5 months in advance. Advance publicity and ticket sales should not exceed 4 to 5 weeks. Allow an hour or two to set up the dance area with decorations and check the sound system. The dance lasts from 7 p.m. until midnight. Cleanup takes an hour.

Expenditures: Allocate $500 seed money to get this project off the ground. Expenses usually involve site rental, honorarium for the "caller," concession items, band, publicity and promotional activities. Many local square-dance organizations will be only too happy to donate their services and expertise for worthy, non-profit organizations which undertake to promote and advance the art of square dancing. Some square-dance advocates are willing to even supply a musical group and a "caller" without cost. Organizers should not be bashful in attempting to obtain equipment and supplies on a donated or greatly reduced basis. Highlight the worthy cause for which this event is being held and publicize how the profits will be put to good use.

Personnel (Staff/Volunteers): A small group of volunteers (5-10) and staff (1-2) are needed to plan and implement this fund raiser. However, the selling of advance tickets should involve a much larger group of helpers (20-30) who should approach their friends, neighbors and co-workers. Securing the services of a professional "caller" (one who is an excellent teacher of novices) is an absolute must. A lively and enthusiastic caller can create an atmosphere in which everyone, both inexperienced and experienced, can enjoy themselves. A square-dance band (2-5 persons) is also necessary.

RISK MANAGEMENT: Legal liability exposure is minimal with full adherence to all of the health and safety regulations pertaining to the concession operation. The downside financial risk is reduced significantly if sufficient advance tickets sales are made. Similarly, if the site is obtained without cost or at a greatly reduced cost, this fund raising project has little financial risk. Check to be sure that the dancers will not damage the surface of the floor that is being danced upon.

PERMITS/LICENSES: If alcohol is sold at the dance it may be necessary to secure an alcohol license. In many communities the existence of the concession stand also requires a permit. Check with the town clerk or local municipal bureau of licenses. Secure permission from managers at local malls and shopping centers prior to placing flyers on vehicles in their lots.

HINTS: Although new square-dance "calls" are being created all the time there is a standardized list of dances for the purpose of instruction, beginning with the very basic of dances to those that are more complicated. Thus, instruction is easily facilitated for the beginning or novice patron. Some groups have piggybacked this type of fund raising effort onto another activity sponsored by the same organization, such as an athletic contest or recreation activity. Door prizes help promote excitement throughout the evening. Once successful, this event can easily become an anticipated annual event.

Fund raiser #16
Weight Loss Marathon

POTENTIAL NET INCOME: $2,500

COMPLEXITY/DEGREE OF DIFFICULTY: Moderate

DESCRIPTION: Adult fans and supporters of a sport program or recreation organization, who also need to lose weight, agree to go on a collective diet over a two- or three-month period. Each of the dieters solicits pledges from individuals and businesses in the community based upon the number of pounds that they will lose during this time period. The pledges can range from 10 cents a pound to a dollar or even more, whatever the market will bear.

SCHEDULING: This community-based fund raising project can be scheduled at any time of the year. However, right after New Year's is an ideal time since the general public is frequently focused on losing some of the pounds gained over the holidays. Also, then the conclusion of the weight loss marathon is right before the summer months.

RESOURCES:

Facilities: A site is needed where dieters can weigh in on a weekly or bi-weekly basis. Also, a large room such as a gymnasium or recreation hall capable of accommodating a large gathering of 50-75 individuals is needed for the final weigh-in and celebration gathering.

Equipment and supplies: Scales, a PA system, flyers, posters, markers, signs, pledge cards and donated prizes and awards should be available.

Publicity and promotion: News articles should appear in the local newspapers and area penny-savers explaining the structure of this unique community fund raising event. Advance announcements via PA systems should be made at other community sporting and recreation activities. Even flyers can be distributed on windshields of vehicles parked at local malls and shopping centers. Local businesses and organizations can also display signs or posters publicizing the weight loss marathon. A large outdoor sign illustrating the amount of pounds lost, on a weekly basis, should be erected on the site of the sponsoring organization. All publicity and promotional efforts should include mention of the fact that this is a fund raising project sponsored by a local non-profit organization for a worthy cause. Highlight how the profits will be spent within the community.

Time: It can take one or two weeks to plan and organize this project and make reservations for the weigh-in site(s). Allow another 4-6 weeks to line up those individuals who will attempt to lose weight and also solicit pledges. The time spent soliciting pledges should be kept to a minimum, no longer than 3-4 weeks. Two or three months can comprise the dieting time period. The final weigh-in should include a fun evening (two to three hours) where individual dieters are weighed in and the amount of money each person has raised is announced.

Expenditures: Allocate $200 in seed money for this fund raiser, most of which will be spent for promotional efforts and the printing of the pledge and explanation sheets.

Personnel (Staff/Volunteers): If a mere 30 volunteers and staff are involved in the weight loss marathon and each averages 10 pounds lost with an average of $30 pledged per pound from 30 individuals, the gross income totals $2,700. Securing local celebrities and influential people to join in the weight loss effort (and pledge solicitation) helps to gain increased publicity for the fund raising project. Additional helpers (5-7) are needed to assist in the weekly weigh-in of the dieters on a rotating basis. A popular master of ceremony helps make the final weigh-in and subsequent awarding of prizes a huge success.

RISK MANAGEMENT: Have someone representing the medical profession (a physician or assistant, nurse or athletic trainer) available to monitor and weigh each volunteer, on a weekly basis. No minors should be involved in this fund raising project, and adults must sign a hold-harmless agreement releasing the organization and its volunteers from liability exposure other than for gross negligence. There is no downside financial risk.

PERMITS/LICENSES: Be sure to secure permission from the managers at the malls and shopping centers before putting flyers on windshields of vehicles parked in their lots.

HINTS: Have a special weigh-in ceremony where each of the volunteer weight losers will have his/her starting weight determined. At the conclusion of the two- or three-month period, there should be another formal weigh-in ceremony where each participant's final weight is determined. Donated awards and prizes can be given to those individuals who have lost the greatest number of pounds, the greatest percentage of their body weight, etc. Other prizes can be earned by dieters who have raised the most money. Don't be surprised if approximately 10 percent of the pledges fail to result in actual cash donations, for whatever reasons. To help keep this percentage as low as possible, provide each solicitor with explanation sheets that can be left with those individuals making pledges. A signed statement at the final weigh-in stating the exact number of pounds lost by each dieter can be given to each donor who made a pledge. This helps to authenticate the whole collection process and greatly increases the percentage of money pledged.

Fund raiser #17
Sport Poster for Sale

POTENTIAL NET INCOME: $2,700

COMPLEXITY/DEGREE OF DIFFICULTY: Low

DESCRIPTION: Permission is secured from a sport celebrity to utilize a unique color photograph of that individual in a team uniform and sport pose. The photo is converted to large (2-1/2 by 3-1/2 feet) posters that the sponsoring sport or recreation organization may then sell to the general public as part of a fund raising project. The posters are sold at a price of at least $8 over and above the actual cost of printing of the posters. Generally speaking, the selling price will be determined by what the market will bear in any given community. And, this in turn is affected by the popularity of the sport celebrity, the economy, the competition, etc.

SCHEDULING: Although this project can be initiated at any time, the actual selling window should be timed to coincide with the sport season and pre-season in which the celebrity competes.

RESOURCES:

Facilities: A site is needed to store posters until sold.

Equipment and supplies: Signs, posters and display tables.

Publicity and promotion: Signs and flyers should be displayed throughout the community promoting the sale of the sport celebrity posters. Announcements in the area news media can highlight the availability of the celebrity posters at sport contests and/or recreational events sponsored by the fund raising organization. Posters can also be sold by local businesses and organizations. The posters can even be sold on a door-to-door basis by volunteers, both by youngsters and adults.

Time: This fund raiser can be planned and organized in less than two weeks. But it may take upwards of 2-3 months to secure the permission of an appropriate sport celebrity to utilize one of their color photographs on the poster. Allow another 3-5 weeks to actually have the posters printed up, ready for sale.

Expenditures: The permission to use a photograph and the actual photographic negative should be received pro bono due to the nature of the non-profit fund raising group. The cost of the posters will vary depending upon the number of posters ordered, the quality of paper, the number of colors, the amount of type, and the size. Plan on spending $500 for the actual printing of 400 posters and another $50 for publicity and promotional costs. Also, if the services of a professional photographer is needed, allocate $200 for this person's expertise.

Personnel (Staff/Volunteers): The most valuable helper or volunteer is the individual who has access to one or more desirable sport celebrities and who can convince a celebrity to permit use of that person's photograph. A group of dedicated volunteers (30) and staff (1-2) is needed to effectively market and sell the posters during the pre-season and early 3-4 weeks of the sport season. If the celebrity does not provide a color photograph but will allow the fund raising entity to take pictures, it is necessary to secure the services of an excellent photographer.

RISK MANAGEMENT: The downside financial risk consists of the money spent for the printing of the 400 posters. To reduce the possibility of unsold posters organizers should attempt to secure permission from a very popular celebrity sport star. Also, the selling of the posters should commence during the pre-season weeks and continue during the early weeks of the sport season or until the supply is depleted. There is always the danger or risk that the sport star or celebrity will be injured or traded before all of the posters can be sold. Also, be sure a secure the celebrity's written permission (sign-off) indicating that the poster (final proof) as presented is approved for sale by the fund raising entity.

PERMITS/LICENSES: Some communities have imposed restrictions on door-to-door selling and require the securing of a hawking or peddling license. Check with the town clerk or other municipal offices in your community.

HINTS: The objective of the fund raising organization should be to secure permission from the most popular sport celebrity for the geographical area in which the posters will be marketed and sold. Of course, if the celebrity will personally autograph selected posters the selling price (value) may double or even triple. It is not wise to skimp on securing the services of a professional photographer if the sponsoring group is responsible for providing the photographer. After all, the right photograph will do wonders while a poor photo will doom the fund raising effort. Remember, the celebrity will always retain the right of refusal of use of any photos taken (as well as the actual look of the final poster). Thus, the photographs had better be expertly taken, developed and printed. Ditto with the creation and final printing of the posters.

Fund raiser #18
50's Sock Hop

POTENTIAL NET INCOME: $3,000

COMPLEXITY/DEGREE OF DIFFICULTY: Moderate

DESCRIPTION: This fund raiser features a dance with the theme of a 1950's Sock Hop, featuring music by a DJ service. Hors d'oeuvres are provided as well as a cash bar. Advance tickets are $20 per person and $25 at the door. Door prizes are awarded for best costumes and for winning various dance contests and "name that tune" games. If 150 individuals purchase tickets the gross income is $3,000 plus whatever is made from the cash bar (estimated $750 net profit). Naturally, a higher ticket price or additional dancers will result in greater profits.

SCHEDULING: The dance should be scheduled on a Friday or Saturday evening.

RESOURCES:

Facilities: A suitable area for dancing at a convenient location with adequate and safe parking is needed. The site could be a gymnasium or a party house catering to large gatherings. The site could also be held outdoors on a parking lot, weather permitting.

Equipment and supplies: Tables and chairs to seat 75% of the number attending the dance. Door prizes and table favors should be solicited from area boosters and businesses. Appropriate decorations are a must.

Publicity and promotion: Promote the sale of advance tickets on the basis of enjoying the music and the dancing of the 1950s coupled with helping a worthy cause. Be sure to publicize how the money raised will be put to good use within the community. Mention of this event in the area news media is important but even more essential is the person-to-person solicitation of potential ticket purchasers and the display of posters and distribution of flyers within the community. The latter can be accomplished by having volunteers distribute flyers (with permission) at area malls and other selected businesses. Finally, encourage group participation from different organizations and businesses.

Time: The dance starts at 8 p.m. and runs until 1 a.m. Planning for this event takes 1-2 weeks. Reserving a facility may have to be done months in advance. Plan on 2 hours for cleanup after the dance.

Expenditures: Securing the services of a popular DJ "record spinner" is essential for this fund raiser. Renting the party house and providing hors d'oeuvres can be an expensive proposition unless the owner gives a special price break to the sponsoring group. The cost of the bartenders is usually figured in with the total cost of renting the facility. Of course, the sock hop can also be held in a large gymnasium with the dancers wearing socks (not shoes) so as to protect the gym floor (just like in high school during the 1950s). Or, the site could even be the parking lot outside the sponsoring group's facility. One caution in terms of using a school or recreational facility: usually alcohol consumption is forbidden. Regardless of the site used, tasteful and appropriate decorations should adorn the facility. Plan on spending between $750 and $1,000 on total expenses. However, expenses can be significantly reduced if services and supplies are obtained on a reduced cost or pro bono basis.

Personnel (Staff/Volunteers): Staff (2-4) and volunteers (25-30) are needed to market the advance tickets and sell tickets at the door. There is a need for 10-15 people to be involved in the dance itself, including site preparation, supervision and cleanup. Staff and volunteers may also serve as bartenders, thus saving money.

RISK MANAGEMENT: The use of designated drivers should be encouraged and the promoters should volunteer to have any ticket purchaser driven home free of charge through the efforts of staff, volunteers or cab drivers who donate their services. The financial risks are minimal as long as the organization reserves the right to cancel the dance without financial obligations to the party house and various personnel if ticket sales are insufficient. If this dance is to become an annual affair, frequently the organizing group is willing to make less profit in the inaugural year in anticipation of increasing profitability in the future, once word gets out about what an enjoyable time everyone had at the initial dance.

PERMITS/LICENSES: If the site is not at a licensed party house, there may be a need to secure a special license to dispense spirits. Check with municipal offices such as the town clerk or the local police department for details.

HINTS: Having someone take photographs of those in attendance with a Polaroid camera and then charging a modest fee (another method of generating profit) can help enhance the enjoyment of the evening for those in attendance. A variation of this fund raiser involves inviting car enthusiasts to display their vehicles outside the facility during the hours of the dance. Or, if the event is being held outside, 1950 vehicles could be parked adjacent to the "dance area." Finally, don't forget to market this dance to local car clubs and associations, especially those affiliated with vehicles of the '50s and '60s.

Fund raiser #19
Quilt Raffle

POTENTIAL NET INCOME: $3,000

COMPLEXITY/DEGREE OF DIFFICULTY: Low

DESCRIPTION: A community raffle is held for a beautiful, 62" by 62" hand-pieced, hand-sewn quilt. Tickets are sold for $5 apiece or three for $10. The drawing of the winning ticket and awarding of the quilt can be planned as a special event, that is, as a stand-alone activity. Or, more likely, the announcement of the winning ticket can be piggybacked along with another community event, such as a dinner, recreation gathering or an athletic contest.

SCHEDULING: The raffle can be scheduled at any time of the year.

RESOURCES:

Facilities: No special facility is needed if the raffle drawing is held as part of another regularly scheduled event in the community.

Equipment and supplies: Signs, posters, markers, camera and film, a storage box for the stubs of tickets sold, a glass bowl (from which to pick the winning ticket), raffle tickets and receipt/record books are required.

Publicity and promotion: Publicity surrounding the raffle consists of newspaper coverage as well as mention by the local radio stations as part of the stations' public service announcements (PSAs). A highly patronized local dining establishment or other popular store can display the actual quilt to be raffled. Local businesses and organizations can also display signs or posters promoting the raffle. Some can even sell raffle tickets on site. Utilize the PA system at sporting events or recreation activities sponsored by the organizing group to help publicize the upcoming raffle. Take a photograph of the winner with the beautiful quilt for possible publication in local newspapers, including area penny-savers.

Time: The raffle can be planned and organized within a week or two. Securing a quality quilt to raffle can take as long as 6 months. Plan on spending at least an hour working with the adult and young volunteers who will help sell the raffle tickets. This is necessary in an effort to teach them the proper way (no hard sell tactics) of soliciting money from potential patrons. The selling window for the raffle tickets should be kept to a maximum of 5-6 weeks. Allow a total of 6-7 weeks for promotional and publicity efforts surrounding the raffle. The actual selection of the winning ticket can be accomplished in as few as five minutes.

Expenditures: This fund raiser can be kicked off with $150 in seed money allocated for promotional and publicity purposes. If the quilt is not donated, be prepared to spend between $300 and $500 (as a discounted price) for a quality quilt. The quilt can be paid for from the proceeds of the raffle tickets.

Personnel (Staff/Volunteers): The one essential person in this fund raising project is the individual who will donate (or sell at a greatly reduced price) the hand-made quilt. Other volunteers (25-30) and staff (1-2) are needed to help plan, organize and implement the raffle. Raffle tickets need to be sold and the actual raffle needs to be held, preferably piggy-backed along with some other activity or gathering. A popular and entertaining master of ceremony should be selected to pick the winning ticket out of the large glass bowl. The ticket pulling should be an exciting and fun-filled experience.

RISK MANAGEMENT: There is little downside financial risk with this type of fund raising activity. This is especially true if the quilt is secured on a donated or greatly reduced cost basis. Similarly, the legal liability exposure is almost non-existent as long as local and state laws governing raffles are complied with. Of course, it is necessary to secure the completed quilt prior to kicking off the ticket sales and publicity efforts.

PERMITS/LICENSES: Since the quilt raffle is a gambling activity it may be necessary to secure local as well as state approval and permission prior to initiating the sale of raffle tickets. Check with the local police authority or the town clerk.

HINTS: Make it very easy for potential patrons to purchase raffle tickets. Have the tickets available at as many sites as feasible. Be sure to highlight the fact that this is a fund raising project sponsored by a non- profit community organization for a worthy cause. Also, publicize how the profits will be put to good use within the community.

Fund raiser #20
Raffle-Auction

POTENTIAL NET INCOME: $3,000

COMPLEXITY/DEGREE OF DIFFICULTY: Moderate

DESCRIPTION: This fund raising effort is based on the dual concept of a raffle and an auction. Specifically, donated items are displayed on tables. Each item is identified by a description and an actual bid price expected, which buyers are required to bid. Next to each item is a small bowl. Individuals wishing to bid (take a chance) on a specific item may purchase tickets from the cashier for that specific dollar amount. The special tickets have two parts, each with an identical series of numbers. The would-be bidder takes one half of the newly purchased ticket and deposits it in the bowl adjacent to the item. At a specific point in time, announced well in advance, the master of ceremony goes to each item and selects (as in a raffle) from the tickets in the bowl. The holder of the matching numbered ticket for that particular item is the successful "bidder" or winner of the item. The same is done for each of the displayed items until all have been claimed by a winner.

SCHEDULING: This fund raiser can be scheduled anytime in the evening or afternoon, on any day of the week. It must be decided whether this fund raiser will exist by itself or will be held in conjunction with another activity. For example, the raffle-auction could be part of a dinner-dance festivity, or as part of a regular auction, or as a pre-game and half-time activity associated with a football or ice hockey game, or as part of an open house event for a new facility.

RESOURCES:

Facilities: Either an indoor facility or an outdoor area may be used. A special site is required to store the items until the date of the event.

Equipment and supplies: The items in most demand are those which will be given away via the raffle-auction. Display tables, adequate portable microphone and sound system as well as a cash box and two-part tickets are also necessary.

Publicity and promotion: All the typical advertising efforts associated with raffles and auctions should be employed. Announcements in the media coupled with distribution of flyers and the display of posters in merchants' windows are productive tactics. Publicity in area newspapers and pennysavers and by the local radio and television stations is also important.

Time: This entire event can be conducted in less than two hours depending upon the number and type of items to be raffled-auctioned off.

Expenditures: Expenses are at a minimum since the items to be given away are donated. Plan on spending less than $50 for promotional materials and supplies.

Personnel (Staff/Volunteers): Dedicated staff (1-2) and volunteers (30-35) will be needed to make this a noteworthy and highly profitable event. These individuals have responsibility for soliciting and collecting items to be raffled-auctioned as well as for organizing, promoting, marketing and implementing the actual event. A talented master of ceremonies who will keep the event interesting, lively and "moving" should be chosen to award the items.

RISK MANAGEMENT: The risks involved in this event are no different than those experienced in other types of raffles and other variations of auctions. One major risk is attracting sufficiently large audiences who are interested in participating. Early effective publicity highlighting the worthwhile purpose for which the event is being held will generate a sufficiently large and motivated audience. The second major risk involves securing, on a donated basis, a sufficient number of quality items for patrons to win. A large number of highly motivated and effective volunteers and staff will insure the securing of a large number of attractive items.

PERMITS/LICENSES: Since the raffle-auction is a form of gambling, the promoters are faced with the task of securing permission from the local offices and/or state agencies that have responsibility for regulating gambling activities and games of chance. Check with the local governmental offices (the town clerk or municipal bureau of licensing) as well as the state office (Gaming Board or Wagering Agency).

HINTS: It is relatively easy to establish a time limit for the event, for example, one, two or three hours. If this event is organized as a stand-alone, concessions can prove to be another profit-making venture. Start early with the solicitation and collection of items to be given away. In soliciting items, don't overlook hotels/motels (Holiday Inns, Ramada Inns, Hyatt Inns, etc.) for certificates for "get-away weekends" as these are highly prized. Similarly, other types of services are equally desirable, such as gift certificates for rounds of golf, flowers, professional car washes, and a whole host of other businesses. And, finally, don't hesitate to emphasize the non-profit and worthwhile nature of the sponsoring organization plus how the profits will be put to good use within the community.

Fund raising projects to generate between $3,000 and $5,000

3

Chapter 3

Fund raising projects to generate between $3,000 and $5,000

Fund raiser #21
Honor Banquet

POTENTIAL NET INCOME: $3,100

COMPLEXITY/DEGREE OF DIFFICULTY: Moderate

DESCRIPTION: A banquet is given in honor of an individual by a recreation or sport organization. Selected individuals are invited to speak of the honoree at the dinner for a period not to exceed three minutes (literally enforced). Profits are realized from the sale of advance tickets that are priced so as to provide $15 net profit per ticket sold (or whatever the market will bear). With 150 paid attendance, the profit (not counting expenses in promotion and publicity or additional income from sponsors) amounts to $2,250. Additional profit results from business sponsorships of the banquet that are secured at $100 each.

SCHEDULING: The banquet can be held on any Friday or Saturday evening.

RESOURCES:

Facilities: A restaurant or party house with accommodations for 200 to 250 participants will suffice. Adequate and safe parking is an absolute must. The organization's own site might also be used but the loss of atmosphere and apparent lack of sophistication is a matter of concern.

Equipment and supplies: Tables and chairs, a head table, microphone and an excellent sound system are required. Also, all food storage, preparation and dispensing equipment and supplies are necessary if the honor banquet is held at the sponsoring entity's own site. Promotional posters and signs are also needed. Invitations, envelopes and postage must be paid for or secured on a pro bono basis. A borrowed computer, laser printer and graphics software will facilitate the creation of a first-class printed program highlighting the honoree's many accomplishments. A program should be provided for each person in attendance. An appropriate award, a framed certificate or memorable plaque should be presented to the honoree. A duplicate may be kept in the organization's facility to honor the individual in perpetuity.

Publicity and promotion: Since the purpose is to provide homage to an outstanding and popular individual in the community, there should be little problem in attracting a large audience. Mailings with special invitations can be made to selected individuals. Group tables can be discounted to businesses and organizations. Signs and posters should be displayed within area businesses. Some businesses and organizations can even serve as ticket outlets. Be sure to seek mention of the event within the area news media, including the various pennysavers.

Time: The event may be planned within 1-2 weeks. Lining up the speakers, the master of ceremony and sponsors can take an additional 2-3 weeks. Advertising and publicity for the event should take place within a 4-5 week period. On the day of the event itself be prepared to spend 2-3 hours getting the site decorated and taking care of last minute details. The banquet starts at 6:30 p.m., with cocktails and dinner following at 7:15 p.m. Cleanup can be completed within 2 hours.

Expenditures: Plan on spending $200 on dinner invitations to be mailed (including postage and envelopes) as well as on promotional and publicity costs. The award, certificate or plaques can total $100. Table decorations can be donated or purchased ($50). Don't be hesitant to ask for donations or reduced costs for anything that is associated with this dinner on the basis of the group's non-profit status and the worthiness of its activities.

Personnel (Staff/Volunteers): A skilled and respected master of ceremony is critical in this type of event when honors and thanks are to be bestowed upon an individual. Volunteers (5-10) and staff (1-2) are needed to obtain business or corporate sponsorships from the community as well as to get the site decorated.

RISK MANAGEMENT: Great care must be taken to insure that this event is perceived as a first-class event. There is little financial risk involved since the pricing of the banquet ticket plus corporate sponsors provide all the upfront money and insure a net profit for the organization. Legal liability is held to a minimum as long as all health and safety regulations are obeyed.

PERMITS/LICENSES: If the banquet is held at a party house or restaurant there is no need to secure any license. If the event is held at the organization's own site, then food and liquor permits may be required. Check with appropriate municipal offices such as the town clerk or health department.

HINTS: This fund raiser can be a very successful affair—both in terms of finances and in terms of positive public relations generated on behalf of the recreation or sport entity. Of course, the banquet can honor more than a single individual. Note that when more persons are being honored there is always a greater number of people desiring to attend. Creating an opportunity to say "thank you" by means of the honor banquet in a truly first class manner can also create positive goodwill for the organization as well as increase the esteem and prestige of the staff and volunteers in the community.

Fund raiser #22
Team Banquet

POTENTIAL NET INCOME: $3,300

COMPLEXITY/DEGREE OF DIFFICULTY: Moderate

DESCRIPTION: A team's banquet is held to honor the athletes for all sports in a season. It differs from the traditional end-of-season food gathering because of the presence of a well-known and popular celebrity to speak after the formal dinner. Everyone (even staff and parents) pays to attend the event, other than the athletes and the celebrity speaker. Soliciting generous benefactors (sponsors) to cover the costs of the meals for the athletes as well as the speaker's fee, if any, is necessary. Only advance tickets are sold. Tickets are priced so as to generate at least $15 profit over the cost of the meal. However, the tickets for the athletes, which are paid for through the generosity of sponsors, are priced at cost (food plus site rental costs, if any). If 125 athletes attend (their meals paid by sponsors), complemented by 250 adults, the profit can be over $3,000, even after all expenses are deducted. Plan on budgeting $200 in seed money.

SCHEDULING: The banquet may be scheduled for any Friday or Saturday evening when there are no major conflicts and when parents and other adults will be likely to attend.

RESOURCES:

Facilities: A large banquet hall, usually available at a party house or restaurant, is required. The site should be capable of seating up to 300-400 individuals. Adequate parking is essential.

Equipment and supplies: Tables, chairs, tickets, PA system, dining paraphernalia, decorations, and individual souvenirs or table favors to give to each athlete. Also, individual athletic awards to be given to outstanding athletes should be prominently displayed.

Publicity and promotion: Intense publicity efforts should be undertaken by volunteers and staff. Promotional efforts should hinge upon the worthy nature of this event (recognizing young athletes) and the non-profit nature of the sponsoring group. Solicitation of potential sponsors and individual ticket purchasers should be organized on a person-to-person basis (face-to-face, phone, writing). Posters and signs should be displayed in area businesses and mention of the banquet should be made by the local news media. Don't forget to use the PA system at other community events. Advance tickets can also be sold by area merchants.

Time: The event can be planned and organized within two weeks. However, plan on making the necessary reservations for the site at least 6-9 months in advance. Likewise, confirming the presence of the speaker, if one is to be involved, should be done well in advance, as early as 6-7 months before the actual banquet. The publicity should run for 5-6 weeks with the selling window for advance tickets restricted to 4-5 weeks.

Expenditures: Plan on spending $200 on publicity and promotional efforts. If the awards are not donated (or sponsored), at least try to obtain a discounted price. Awards should not exceed $200. The rental cost of the facility is usually built into the total cost of the dinner or banquet and can be paid for from advance ticket sales and sponsor contributions. Allocate up to $250 for an outstanding speaker (sports celebrity), if not obtained for free.

Personnel (Staff/Volunteers): Volunteers (25) and staff (1-2) must be effective in soliciting sponsors to pay for the meals of the athletes as well as marketing and selling the tickets to parents, fans and the general public. A skilled and experienced master of ceremony is a must.

RISK MANAGEMENT: If a large restaurant or party house is used there is little liability exposure in terms of the storage, preparation, and serving of food. Similarly, the financial risks are greatly diminished if sufficient advance tickets are sold and if adequate sponsors are obtained. For each athlete in attendance, count on at least 1.3 adults to also attend. Add fans, coaches and athletic administrators, members of the booster club (if one exists) and others from the community and the total attendance (and profit) becomes significant.

PERMITS/LICENSES: No special permits or licenses are required if a regular eating establishment (restaurant or party house) is chosen for the banquet. There may be a need for a permit or license if the dinner is scheduled for a gymnasium or other facility not normally used to serve food.

HINTS: The banquet concept need not be limited to sports teams. Recreation organizations and other groups can be equally effective in implementing a successful fund raising project which revolves around a banquet and solicitation of sponsors to help pay for the costs of the meal and use of the facility. Once this type of banquet has been successful, subsequent banquets in succeeding years will be easier to plan, organize and implement since a significant number of the adults who were in attendance in previous years will know what to expect. Naturally, all athletes are required to attend since their presence helps to insure that their parents and other supportive individuals will attend (as paying customers).

Fund raiser #23
Family Portraits

POTENTIAL NET INCOME: $3,400

COMPLEXITY/DEGREE OF DIFFICULTY: Low

DESCRIPTION: Individual and family color portraits are taken for a reasonable price with the gross proceeds divided (60/40 split) between the sponsoring organization and the professional photographer. Gross revenue of $6,000 generates $3,400, after expenses, for the non-profit group.

SCHEDULING: The photo session can be scheduled for any Saturday. If the site is at a mall or shopping center or large department store, try to pick a busy shopping day to take advantage of heavy foot traffic. There needs to be a second day scheduled when the customers may come and retrieve the finished photographs.

RESOURCES:

Facilities: Almost any facility will do. However, the photography sessions might also be located in the lobby of a large mall, shopping center or within a department store. The key is to select a site that will be convenient. Heavy foot and vehicular traffic is an absolute must. The site could also be at the sponsoring group's own facility—before, during and after a sport contest or recreation activity.

Equipment and supplies: All of the photographic supplies and equipment (camera, film, photographic paper, chemicals, background screens, lights, toys, etc.) should be provided by the photographer. A table, chairs, receipt book, order forms and a cash box (with change) must be available at the site. Signs, posters and flyers should be created to help in promoting and publicizing the fund raising project.

Publicity and promotion: Extensive advance publicity should be conducted 3-5 weeks in advance of the actual photo session. Be sure to highlight the facts that (1) a professional photographer will be taking the photos, (2) the sponsor of this project is a non-profit, local organization, and (3) how the proceeds from this fund raiser will be used (be specific) to help pay for worthy projects within the community. Advertisements and announcements in area news media (including local penny-savers) are a must. Perhaps free radio and television spots might help publicize this fund raiser due to its non-profit nature. Flyers can be placed on the windshields of vehicles parked in area malls and shopping centers. A special large sign should be prominently displayed near the area where the portraits are taken.

Time: This fund raising project can be planned and organized within a week. Confirming the location of the photographic session and coming to agreement with a professional photographer can take much longer. Allow 3-4 weeks. The actual photo sessions should be scheduled from 9 a.m. to 8 p.m. on a Saturday to accommodate parents and their children. The finished photographs may be picked up on a publicized subsequent date at the same site between the hours of noon and 5 p.m.

Expenditures: The use of the site should be secured on a donated basis. Plan on spending $200 for promotional and publicity activities and other supplies.

Personnel (Staff/Volunteers): The key is to secure the services of a professional photographer who will agree to split the gross income with the non-profit sponsoring organization. Volunteers (15-20) and staff (1-2) will be needed to help promote and publicize the event as well as to staff the booth where the photographs are to be taken. Additional helpers (5-7) will be needed on the subsequent date to distribute the photos to the customers.

RISK MANAGEMENT: There is little financial risk due to the fact that the photographer receives a percentage of the gross sales and the customers pay for the photos at the initial sitting. Similarly, legal exposure is minimal as long as the pictures are indeed produced and are given to the customers. Of course, the photographs must be of a sufficiently high quality to be worth the price being charged. It is important that the money be immediately deposited in the organization's bank account and that only responsible adults handle the cash or checks.

PERMITS/LICENSES: Permission must be obtained from the mall, shopping center or department store for the two dates when the photo session and the subsequent distribution of photos are to be held. Also, be sure to secure permission from the mall or shopping center's management before placing flyers on vehicles' windshields.

HINTS: Have a clear, firm written agreement with the photographer in terms of what is expected and when the photographs are to be made available to customers. The advantages accruing to the photographer, in addition to some additional profit, is the added exposure to the general public and close association with the highly respected, non-profit organization. It helps if the photographer is a close friend and/or booster of the sponsoring entity in that such an individual is more willing to take a smaller percentage of the gross. Nevertheless, at least 50% of payment due to the photographer should be made only after all of the photographs are made available to the customers. Be prepared for unclaimed photos. In this event, a phone call must be placed to inform each individual that the photos may be picked up at the facility of the sponsoring organization during normal business hours. An added incentive is to schedule a celebrity (sport or otherwise) during certain hours of the session and allow the customers to have their photographs or portraits taken with the celebrity.

Fund raiser #24
Car Bash

POTENTIAL NET INCOME: $3,500

COMPLEXITY/DEGREE OF DIFFICULTY: Low

DESCRIPTION: Advance and on-site tickets are sold for the right to take a sledgehammer to bash a car or truck. The cost of swinging the sledgehammer will be vary depending upon what item(s) on the car is(are) to be broken. For example, to attempt to break a single windshield might cost the swinger $25 while the cost to hit away at a window might be only $10 or $15. To break a headlight or taillight might cost the aggressor $5 or $10 for each swing. Once all of the glass on the vehicle is broken, all subsequent swings are $2 each or three tries for $5. It doesn't take long for the sponsoring group to net $3,500.

SCHEDULING: The car bash can take place at any time of the year, preferably a weekend. The event can be a stand-alone event or can be held in conjunction with an athletic event or recreational activity.

RESOURCES:

Facilities: Any outdoor site such as a parking lot will suffice. Ideally, the car bash will be in close proximity to heavily traveled walkways and/or streets in order to attract passersby.

Equipment and supplies: A junker vehicle, a tow truck, sledgehammers, protective eyewear, signs, poster, flyers, trash barrels, brooms, dust pan, tickets, and a cash box are necessary.

Publicity and promotion: This fun activity should be promoted within all of the news media, both print and electronic. Use the PA system at other athletic contests or recreation activities sponsored by the organizing group to promote the event. Local businesses and organizations can display signs and posters. Some can even sell advance tickets. Flyers or handbills can be placed on the windshields of vehicles parked in area malls or shopping centers.

Time: The time required to organize this fund raising project is very minimal, one or two days. It may take a week or so to locate and secure a suitable junker vehicle to be demolished. Allow 3-4 weeks to publicize the car bash and to sell advance tickets. Moving the car from the junkyard to the site of the "bashing" can take an hour. Cleaning up the site after the event can take an hour or two while moving the beaten wreck back to the junkyard can take another hour. The car bash can be an all-day event, from 9 a.m. to early evening.

Expenditures: The junk car or truck can be purchased for $50. Allocate another $50 for promotional and publicity materials. The use of the tow truck to move the junker should be secured on a loan basis.

Personnel (Staff/Volunteers): Volunteers (10) and staff (1-2) are needed to organize the car bash, to secure the vehicle, to have it moved to the site of the "bashing," to sell advance and on-site tickets, and to clean up the site afterwards and return the vehicle to the junk yard.

RISK MANAGEMENT: It is extremely important that spectators be sufficiently far away from the vehicle that they are not injured by flying glass or metal. Similarly, those individuals swinging the sledgehammer must wear protective eyewear. Be sure that the site is completely cleaned of glass, metal and other debris.

PERMITS/LICENSES: None unless a concession stand is operated. In that event, a temporary permit might be required. Check with the town clerk or other municipal office. If flyers or handbills are placed on vehicles' windshields at shopping centers, secure permission from the manager of the mall or shopping center.

HINTS: Try to secure a junk vehicle that has the windows as well as the head and taillights intact. These are the first to be broken and the organizers should charge more for the privilege of breaking glass than merely denting a door. This fund raising project can become more involved if a concession stand is operated by the organizing group.

Fund raiser #25
Donkey Basketball Competition

POTENTIAL NET INCOME: $3,500

COMPLEXITY/DEGREE OF DIFFICULTY: Moderate

DESCRIPTION: A modified game of basketball is played on an indoor court by individuals while riding donkeys, which wear special padding on their hooves. The donkeys and a visiting team can be hired to travel to your community to play against a local all-star team by contacting one of two professional fund raising companies that provide donkey basketball competition. Buckeye Donkey Ball Company, P.O. Box 314, Westerville, Ohio 43081, is one such team. Profit is generated through the sale of advance tickets, and tickets sold on the day of the event and from the sale of concession items and souvenirs.

SCHEDULING: Promoted as a fun, family-oriented event, the donkey basketball competition is usually held on a Friday evening or Saturday afternoon or evening.

RESOURCES:

Facilities: An indoor basketball court is needed.

Equipment and supplies: Special padding, provided by the visiting team, is required for the donkeys so as to provide much needed protection for the hardwood floor/court. Souvenirs and concession inventory are necessary if such sales are to take place. Tickets, cash boxes and posters must be secured. Donated prizes to be given away before and during the exhibition can be obtained from local businesses.

Publicity and promotion: The basketball contest can be advertised and promoted as unique family entertainment involving competition between hometown favorites or celebrities against visitors, all riding on donkeys. The donkey basketball fund raiser should be promoted within the area news media. Local businesses and organizations can play a significant part in publicizing this event by displaying signs and posters. Some can even serve as ticket outlets for advance sales. The advertisements and publicity should highlight the various prizes and giveaways that will be part of the festivities.

Time: Plan on spending up to four weeks to plan and organize this fund raiser. However, it may be necessary to confirm the exact date of the future competition as early as 4-8 months in advance. The actual competition takes approximately 30-45 minutes.

Expenditures: There is an up-front cost for hiring the visiting opponents (including the animals); other expenses will revolve around publicity efforts and securing inventory for concessions and souvenirs sales. Expect to spend $500 on seed money for this fund raiser.

Personnel (Staff/Volunteers): Approximately 20-30 volunteers and staff will be needed to help sell advance and day of event tickets, staff the souvenir and concession staff, assist with the parking, and to clean up following the contest.

RISK MANAGEMENT: Contact an insurance agency to investigate the need for special liability insurance. The donkey company will carry insurance, but it is wise to have an expert examine the existing coverage of both the donkey company and the sponsoring organization and make a recommendation about additional coverage. Expect the donkey company to provide a bond of sufficient amount and to hold harmless the sponsoring organization as well as the individuals associated with the organization, as well as the owner of the facility where the donkey competition takes place. It is imperative that all health regulations are met in terms of the treatment of the donkeys. This includes transportation, housing, general treatment and medical care of the animals. Of late, some representatives of the National Society for the Prevention of Cruelty to Animals (NSPCA) have been especially critical of the use of animals in any type of fund raising or promotional effort. Carefully weigh the pros and cons, the financial advantages versus the potential risks, before committing to this type of fund raising effort. With advance ticket sales, the financial risks are few.

PERMITS/LICENSES: All health regulations relating to the treatment and care of the animals must be met. Representatives of the local health department as well or a local veterinarian can advise the organizers whether or not any special permits or licenses or proof of vaccination of the donkeys are required. Check the local health department or municipal offices to determine whether a permit is needed for the concession stand.

HINTS: The donkey basketball contest may be organized as a stand-alone event or be piggy-backed (precede or follow) onto another activity such as a regularly scheduled recreation activity or athletic contest. The success of this fund raiser rests in the sponsoring group's ability to sell sufficient advance tickets. It may be wise to arbitrarily select a cutoff date at which the organizers may cancel the proposed contest without incurring any financial commitment to the donkey basketball company.

Fund raiser #26
Dunking Booth

POTENTIAL NET INCOME: $3,500 annually

COMPLEXITY/DEGREE OF DIFFICULTY: Moderate

DESCRIPTION: The dunking booth can be set up at each home football, baseball or soccer game. Patrons get to throw a baseball at a target, 10 inches in diameter, from a distance of 35 feet. Each throw costs $1 or 7 throws for $5. If struck, the target releases a mechanism that dumps whomever is sitting on the platform into a large container of water. If only $100 profit is realized each time the dunking booth is set up, the annual net profit can easily approach $3,500 if the booth is piggybacked onto only 35 sporting events during the year.

SCHEDULING: This outdoor fund raising activity can be scheduled any time when the weather is reasonably warm. To insure high foot traffic it is wise to schedule the dunking booth around an outside sporting event.

RESOURCES:

Facilities: The dunking booth can be set up in any space that measures 50 feet by 20 feet. It is most important that the site be in close proximity to the athletic event, perhaps adjacent to the ticket booths or the entrances to the facility. In such an event, everyone who buys a ticket or who enters the game will have to pass the dunking booth.

Equipment and supplies: Tables, chairs, a canvas backdrop (to stop missed balls), rope, posters, signs, tickets and a cash box are all required and should be obtained on a free or loan basis. Materials for a dunking booth can be donated and the booth built by volunteers.

Publicity and promotion: There must be adequate signs on site to attract those attending a game or event. A portable PA system should be utilized to publicize the dunking booth and promote its patronage. Even the main PA system for the athletic event can help publicize and promote the dunking booth. Be sure to announce and publicize the name of the person sitting on the "dunking seat." Advance publicity should be garnered in the local press. Area businesses can display signs or posters.

Time: The planning and organization for this fund raising project can be completed in less than a week. Allow 3-4 weeks to construct the portable booth with the dunking mechanism and target arm. The booth should be able to be set up within an hour or two and dismantled in an hour. The dunking booth should be open for business at least an hour prior to the athletic event and stay open until there are no more paying customers.

Expenditures: The cost of constructing the portable dunking booth should be minimal, if anything at all. This is because donations of materials as well as labor should be sought by the fund raising group. If the group elects to purchase a professionally built dunking booth, allocate between $2,500 to $3,500, plus delivery. Allocate $200 in seed money for signs, posters and other promotional efforts.

Personnel (Staff/Volunteers): Volunteers (10-15) and staff (1-2) are needed to plan, organize and promote this fund raising project. Additional volunteers are needed to set up and dismantle the booth. Still other brave hearts need to be willing to perch on the "dunking seat." They may be local celebrities such as the mayor, police or fire chief, members of the city council, staff members of the sponsoring organization, teachers, coaches, sport or educational administrators, parents, etc.

RISK MANAGEMENT: There can be a sizeable financial risk if a professionally constructed dunking booth needs to be purchased. However, if the organizers build their own with donated materials and labor, this risk evaporates. To reduce the legal liability exposure of the organizers and the sponsoring group, it is wise to have an attorney draw up a hold-harmless agreement to be signed by those who sit on the "dunking seat."

PERMITS/LICENSES: None.

HINTS: Dress up volunteers on the "dunking seat" in special T-shirts, shorts and funny hats. Encourage them to egg-on or entice potential "throwers" to buy (more) tickets in an effort to dunk the "mouth." Those volunteers should be rotated every hour lest they become overly chilled or worn out. Following the year's fund raising efforts, a special food gathering might be planned at which all of the volunteers would be recognized and rewarded with special awards and/or appreciation plaques(donated by local businesses).

Fund raiser #27
Fall Flower Bulb Sale

POTENTIAL NET INCOME: $3,500

COMPLEXITY/DEGREE OF DIFFICULTY: Moderate

DESCRIPTION: Flower bulbs are sold to fans, friends, supporters and the general public. Orders are taken for a specific number and type of bulbs that can be planted in the fall for spring flowering. The bulbs are then ordered from a wholesaler at a prearranged price. Volunteers of the sponsoring organization deliver the bulbs to the purchasers and collect the money.

SCHEDULING: This fund raising project takes place in the early fall.

RESOURCES:

Facilities: The only facility needed will be a place to unload and to briefly store the bulbs received from the wholesaler before redistribution to the volunteer sales/delivery force and final delivery to the purchasers.

Equipment and supplies: Receipt and record books are needed to keep track of orders. Additionally, poster boards, paper and paint with which to create signs are also required. And donated prizes to be awarded to top salespersons need to be solicited.

Publicity and promotion: Announcements in area newspapers and penny-savers coupled with flyers and posters displayed in the windows of area merchants can be most effective. Some businesses can even take orders. Of course nothing substitutes for actual one-on-one, person-to-person solicitation, whether it be face to face, via the mail by means of a personal letter, or over the phone. One-on-one solicitation coupled with word of mouth advertisement and free publicity form the core of the marketing efforts. Frequently, parents of the youngsters involved take flyers to work and take orders there, thus significantly expanding the pool of potential purchasers and increasing profits.

Time: Planning for this event can take 1-2 weeks. The actual selling "window" for the bulbs consists of 3-4 weeks during September and October, depending upon location. Allow a week for receipt of the bulbs from the wholesaler. The bulbs sold can then be distributed (and money collected) within 1-3 days. The entire fund raising effort can easily be concluded within 5-7 weeks.

Expenditures: The costs of the bulbs can be paid for from the proceeds of the sale, after the money is collected. Anticipate a 40%-50% markup (or whatever the market will bear) on the bulbs. Initial advertising, promotional and sales materials will run less than $100.

Personnel (Staff/Volunteers): The entire fund raising effort can be implemented by 1-2 staff and 30-35 volunteers. The latter, organized into teams, will compete to sell the greatest number of bulbs. Prizes (donated) can be given to the teams and individuals who are the "best" salespersons. Provide adult supervision of any youngsters attempting to sell the bulbs.

RISK MANAGEMENT: There are really no downside financial risks in this type of fund raiser since the bulbs are not ordered until a purchaser indicates a firm commitment to buy them. If a would-be purchaser subsequently reneges on the order (or moves out of town), the promoters merely attempt to sell the left-over bulbs to other purchasers, who might want an extra bulb or two. To reduce liability exposure, there should be an orientation session for the youngsters doing the selling. This is the opportunity to present selling hints and safety suggestions as well as to point out that no one should attempt to sell at night or in unfamiliar neighborhoods without an adult present.

PERMITS/LICENSES: A peddler's or hawker's permit might be required in some communities. The office of town clerk or the general municipal offices will be a good source of information regarding required permits or licenses.

HINTS: This fund raiser can become an annual event and may result in big profits for the sponsoring organization if the sales force is adept at marketing the product. Advertising a money-back guarantee for bulbs that do not bloom will help provide credibility. In reality, very few (if any) individuals will ever take advantage of this offer. However, advertising such a guarantee is a public relations plus.

Fund raiser #28
Fish Fry Fund raising Dinner

POTENTIAL NET INCOME: $3,500

COMPLEXITY/DEGREE OF DIFFICULTY: Moderate

DESCRIPTION: This fund raiser is based upon a traditional fish fry. Contributors buy a fish dinner (baked, broiled or fried) which includes cole slaw, french fries, bread, pie and choice of beverage. The food is prepared and cooked by parents and supporters associated with the sport or recreation program. Tickets should be priced so that there is a net profit of $5 per person, excluding promotional and publicity expenses. Tickets are sold both at the door as well as in advance, at a slight discount. If 750 individuals purchase fish dinners, the potential profit is around $3,750, excluding publicity and promotional costs.

SCHEDULING: The fish fry is held on a Friday afternoon and evening anytime during the year. In some communities the early weeks of Lent are an especially popular time for this fund raiser.

RESOURCES:

Facilities: A large indoor or outdoor facility capable of seating 150 to 200 at a time. Suitable parking is an absolute must.

Equipment and supplies: The usual kitchen equipment and supplies are musts in this type of fund raiser. Similarly, adequate tables and chairs as well as trash bins are required, as well as paper plates, cups, napkins, and plastic utensils. A cash box, with $150 in change, a receipt book and a record book are all required. Of course, appropriate decorations are a nice touch.

Publicity and promotion: The advertising and promotional activities should begin some 4-6 weeks in advance of the actual date. This fund raising event should be publicized through all of the normal channels including, but not limited to, notices placed in businesses, announcements made at churches, at schools, at service club meetings and other community events, news items in area papers and over the radio, and flyers mailed or distributed throughout the area. Don't forget about placing flyers on vehicles parked in area malls and shopping centers. Also, the worthiness of the non-profit sponsoring group and how the sport or recreation program will profit from the monies raised should be emphasized.

Time: Planning for this event can be completed within two weeks. Set-up and site preparation can take as long as 4-8 hours. The fish fry itself begins at 2 p.m. and runs until 10 p.m. Anticipate spending several hours cleaning up after the event.

Expenditures: The secret of making big money through this type of fund raiser is to secure those items to be sold on a FREE BASIS—as well as food, drink and paper/plastic items, etc. Similarly, the use of the facility should be on a pro bono basis if possible. Of course, using the organization's own facility eliminates rental costs. Allocate $250 to get this fund raiser off the ground, including promotional and publicity expenses.

Personnel (Staff/Volunteers): There should be at least 40-50 volunteers and 2-3 staff willing to help with the food preparation, as well as the serving of food and cleaning of tables. Of course, selling of tickets, both advance and at the door, is a major responsibility. Staffing should be staggered, thereby always having fresh and energetic people in key positions of responsibility. It is imperative that experienced and skilled cooks be on duty at all times. Don't expect volunteers to work more than 3-4 hours straight. Volunteers and staff should be organized into various committees, that is, site preparation, food and drink, publicity, cleanup, ticket sales, etc. Assign 10-12 well respected individuals to secure food and drink items as well as paper goods and decorations, etc., at a reduced cost.

RISK MANAGEMENT: There are essentially two areas of risk in this type of fund raising effort. First, not attracting sufficient numbers of people to the fish fry. Second, there is always the risk that something will go wrong with the food itself, i.e., the food might be improperly prepared or spoiled. In the first situation, a large number of advance sales can significantly reduce the risk of financial failure. And experienced and knowledgeable cooks should prevent the second catastrophe. If the food or service is inadequate, word of mouth will destroy this fund raiser's future.

PERMITS/LICENSES: Municipal permits or licenses may be necessary in terms of the preparation and dispensing of the food. Fire regulations must be strictly adhered to, including those which restrict the number of individuals within an indoor facility at any one time. Some communities prohibit or restrict the distribution of flyers on vehicles at malls. Check with the local municipal offices for any such regulations.

HINTS: Phone-in and take-out orders should also be extensively advertised. Delivery service might even be available. The fish fry can become an annual or a repeatable fund raising event if the patrons truly enjoy themselves.

Fund raiser #29
Marching Band Competition

POTENTIAL NET INCOME: $3,500

COMPLEXITY/DEGREE OF DIFFICULTY: Moderate.

DESCRIPTION: Invitations are extended to 15-20 different marching bands to compete against one another for awards and prizes. Numerous prizes in the form of team trophies and individual awards are given in several categories. Profits are realized through: (1) entrance fee of $25 per team, (2) admission of $1 per person, (3) corporate or business sponsorships ($200 each) as well as (4) a concessions stand. Anticipate between 750 and 1500 paying spectators consisting of parents, friends and supporters of the youngsters marching in the various bands as well as interested members of the general public. The number of marching band members should number 1000-1200.

SCHEDULING: The event takes place in the fall on a Saturday morning and/or afternoon or a Sunday afternoon.

RESOURCES:

Facilities: A football-sized field. In fact, a football stadium is an ideal facility due to the fact that there is sufficient seating for the paying audience and usually adequate parking. There are usually suitable concession facilities available to boot. If the competition is in the evening, lights must be available.

Equipment and supplies: An excellent loud speaker system is a must. All appropriate concession equipment and supplies must be available. Advance publicity signs and posters must be created as well as special signs to be displayed at the site of the competition acknowledging the corporate/business sponsors. A special printed program containing informative data about each of the competing teams and sponsors should be created and distributed free of charge to all those in attendance. Donated trophies and other awards are secured from businesses and individuals.

Publicity and promotion: The pitch to potential business and corporate sponsors should be based on the worthiness of the fund raising project. This involves sharing with potential sponsors how the money generated from this fund raiser will be put to use within the community. Similarly, point out to the would-be sponsors how their involvement will be good for their businesses in terms of visibility and their association with high school youngsters and their parents. The marching band competition is publicized and promoted within each community sending a competing team. Posters and signs are displayed within businesses and flyers are placed on windshields of vehicles parked in shopping centers and malls. Announcements within area news media are a great help.

Time: Planning for the event can be completed within two weeks. However, securing firm commitments of various marching bands to take part in the competition can take several months. Cleanup can take 1-2 hours.

Expenditures: Plan on spending $200 on promotional efforts. An additional $100 should be anticipated to cover the costs (if any) of the printing of 1500 programs for the event. With the ever-increasing popularity of computers, printers and desk top publishing software, it should not be difficult to print an appropriate program. Ideally even the site could be obtained without cost. Free use of a nearby college's stadium, parking areas, sound system, and the concession facility should be sought on the basis of the recruiting advantages for that institution in terms of having more than 1000 potential college students and their parents on the college campus.

Personnel (Staff/Volunteers): Five to seven skilled and experienced judges are needed to evaluate the bands' performances. Additional volunteers (5- 7) and staff (1-2) are needed to approach corporations and businesses to seek their sponsorship. Help (15-20) with concessions is also needed.

RISK MANAGEMENT: There is little financial risk to the sponsoring organization since firm commitments and entrance fees are obtained from the participating marching bands. The securing of business and corporate sponsors (5-10) also precludes the possibility of any financial loss.

PERMITS/LICENSES: There may be a need for a special food permit to operate the concession stand. Check with the local health department or town clerk.

HINTS: In different sections of the country it might be more appropriate to invite drum and bugle corps to be involved in similar competition. Or, a cheerleading competition involving any number (15-25) of visiting teams might also be appropriate. Unlike marching bands and cheerleading teams, drum and bugle corps do not always exclusively represent individual schools.

Fund raiser #30
Murder Mystery Dinner Party

POTENTIAL NET INCOME: $3,500

COMPLEXITY/DEGREE OF DIFFICULTY: Moderate

DESCRIPTION: Following a formal dinner, preselected guests act out (role-play) a make-believe period murder. Those attending wear costumes indicative of the period of time in which the "murder" occurs. The task facing the guests is to discern which of the actors committed the murder. A variety of clues are created and disseminated to the paying guests. Dinner is planned for a minimum of 50 individuals, and is priced to generate a net profit of $75 over the cost of the meal. Advanced reservations are required. An original script is either created by the organizers or a commercially produced "murder theme party kit" is used.

SCHEDULING: The dinner party may be scheduled Friday or Saturday evening. It is important to select a date that will not be in competition with other popular events held within the community.

RESOURCES:

Facilities: The mystery murder dinner can be held in any restaurant, party house or other facility that can accommodate a large group for dinner. The site should be centrally located with adequate and safe parking.

Equipment and supplies: Appropriate decorations, a script for each of the role-players, special invitations, signs, posters, tickets and a selection of clues should be available. Individual guests provide their own costumes and paraphernalia.

Publicity and promotion: The publicity should specify the period of time in which the so-called "murder" takes place so that all of the guests will be able to wear appropriate costumes for the dinner and the subsequent murder-solving party. Advance publicity should be sent to the area news media, both print and electronic. Local businesses and organizations can display signs and posters. Don't forget to highlight the non-profit nature of the sponsoring organization and how the profits will be used within the community.

Time: The murder mystery party can be planned within 2-3 weeks. Writing the script can take longer, 3-4 weeks. Or, a commercial "murder theme party kit" can be purchased in a single day at many specialty book stores. Selling the tickets to the dinner party should be limited to 3-4 weeks of concentrated effort. The event itself can start with cocktails at 6:30 p.m., followed at 7 p.m. by the sit-down dinner. At 8:30 p.m. the murder mystery tableau can take place either at the dining tables or in another room.

Expenditures: A commercially produced "theme murder kit" can be purchased for less than $40. Allocate $100 for promotional and publicity purposes including signs, posters and tickets. Clues and invitations can be obtained for $100.

Personnel (Staff/Volunteers): Volunteers (10-15) and staff (1-2) are needed to attend the dinner and to serve as actors in the murder mystery. Some of these same individuals as well as other helpers (10-12) are needed as advance ticket sellers within the community. Also, they should invite friends, neighbors and associates to take part in the evening's festivities. Tickets can best be sold on a face to face, person to person basis. A popular master of ceremonies can be most helpful. If an original script is to be written, some of these same volunteers, helpers and staff can play an important role in creating an intriguing and entertaining murder mystery.

RISK MANAGEMENT: If the dinner is at a restaurant or party house, there should be minimal risk in terms of an inadequate or unsafe meal. The financial risk is greatly reduced by the sale of advance tickets. It is imperative that the ticket campaign be successful. The sale of tickets is facilitated by involving as many as 10-15 of the guests (and in some instances, all of the guests) as role-playing actors.

PERMITS/LICENSES: No special permits or licenses are needed if the dinner is held at a commercial eating establishment.

HINTS: It is important to create a suitable atmosphere for the dinner and the subsequent "murder." Some organizers attempt to involve every guest (all 50) as role players in acting out the mystery. Other promoters utilize only preselected volunteers, who also are paying guests at the dinner, for acting out the various roles. The mystery dinner party can easily become an annual affair if the initial gathering is viewed as a success. Positive comments by those in attendance (word of mouth advertisement) can do wonders to promote the event in each subsequent year.

Fund raiser #31
Raffle of a Collectible

POTENTIAL NET INCOME: $3,500

COMPLEXITY/DEGREE OF DIFFICULTY: Moderate

DESCRIPTION: A valuable collectible is secured either via a donation or through a purchase and subsequently raffled–locally and/or through a national effort. A collectible comes about when a company retires a piece from current production and no longer manufactures or sells the item. Such a company is Department 56 located in Eden Prairie, Minnesota 55344-1456 (P.O. Box 44456). This corporation produces a wide variety of miniature porcelain buildings and figurines. A now-discontinued building, the Cathedral Church of St. Marks, which is a part of a set of buildings called "Christmas in the City," is currently worth over $3,000 to collectors on the secondary market.

SCHEDULING: This fund raiser may be initiated at any time of the year.

RESOURCES:

Facilities: No special facility is needed. However, a meeting room may be used to plan and implement the fund raiser as well as a site to draw the winning raffle ticket.

Equipment and supplies: A collectible item to raffle, tickets, envelopes, stamps, signs and posters.

Publicity and promotion: The raffle can be promoted and publicized locally through announcements and advertisements in the area news media as well as by posters and signs displayed in local businesses. On the national level, announcements of the raffle can be placed (free) in any number of national publications devoted to these types of collectibles. There are literally thousands of interested collectors who subscribe to these periodicals. Three such publications are: (1) Dickens' Exchange, Inc., 700 Phosphor Ave., Suite C, Metairie, LA 70005, (2) The Village Chronicle, 200 Post Road # 311, Warwick, RI 02888-1535, and (3) What the Dickens, 2885 W. Ribera Place, Tucson, AZ 85741.

Time: This fund raiser can be planned and organized in a week. However, allow 4-6 weeks to sell the raffle tickets if the promotion is local and 6-8 weeks if the raffle effort is to extend nationally.

Expenditures: If the collectible must be purchased by the sponsoring group, the cost can range between $1,000-$2,500 or more. Plan on spending $150 in seed money for promotional materials, including tickets and mailing costs.

Personnel (Staff/Volunteers): Volunteers (15) and staff (1-2) can be ticket sellers as well as promote the raffle.

RISK MANAGEMENT: To prevent a situation in which the collectible costs $2,500 and only $1,500 is generated through the sale of raffle tickets, the sponsoring organization can place a statement on the back of each raffle ticket that the raffle will be cancelled if insufficient tickets are sold. Another option is to secure a booster or backer to agree to make up any financial loss. Of course, if the volunteers and staff are hardworking, the moving of sufficient tickets should not be a great concern.

PERMITS/LICENSES: Check with the local town clerk or other municipal offices to determine whether a special permit or license is needed.

HINTS: When publicizing the raffle on a national level, it is imperative that a statement is included in all announcements that winners do not have to be present to win. Also, a specific date needs to be publicized when the winning ticket is to be drawn. Publicize the fact that the raffle is being sponsored by a non-profit organization and that the proceeds from the fund raiser will be put to a worthy cause within the community.

Fund raiser #32
Tie-a-Thon

POTENTIAL NET INCOME: $3,500

COMPLEXITY/DEGREE OF DIFFICULTY: Low

DESCRIPTION OF PROJECT: Beautiful ties with the organization's colors and logo (or other suitable design) are sold on a take-order basis to fans, supporters, members of the booster club and to the general public. Several weeks after orders are taken and the money collected, the individual salespersons deliver the ties, which are sold for an $8 net profit or for whatever the market will bear.

SCHEDULING STRATEGIES: This fund raising activity can be scheduled at any time of the year. If door-to-door sales are to be initiated the selling activity should be planned during a time when good weather is expected.

RESOURCES:

Facilities: No special facilities are needed.

Equipment and supplies: Order forms, posters, signs and flyers are all needed. Also, the wholesaler should be able to provide sample ties for potential purchasers to view. If sample ties are not available, the manufacturer should be able to provide printed brochures or flyers with color photos of them. Donated prizes should be solicited to give to top sellers in different age categories.

Publicity and promotion: Ask local businesses and organizations to display signs or posters publicizing the tie sale. Some businesses can even take orders. Announcements should also be made by local newspapers, including the area penny-savers. Don't forget to promote this fund raising project through the use of the PA system at other athletic contests or events. Be sure to always highlight the fact that this is a worthwhile fund raising project sponsored by a non-profit community based organization. Also, share how the profits from this fund raiser will be put to good use.

Time: This fund raising project can be planned within a week. It may take 1-2 weeks to select a wholesaler to provide the ties and to finalize the exact style, colors, the design and the placement of the logo. The publicity and selling window should not extend beyond three to four weeks. Allow two or three weeks for the delivery of the ties from the manufacturer or wholesaler once the total order has been placed. Once the ties are received, they should be delivered within 2-3 days.

Expenditures: Plan on spending $200 to kick off this fund raising project, most of which will be spent for promotional efforts. All prizes should be donated.

Personnel (Staff/Volunteers): The key to this fund raiser is in securing a sufficient number of volunteers (35-50) and staff (2-4) who are dedicated and skilled at selling the ties. Some sponsoring groups organize them into teams which then compete against one another. Assign a responsible adult(s) to oversee the financial records, the ordering of the ties as well as the handling of the money.

RISK MANAGEMENT: Since no orders are placed with the manufacturer until the money is collected, there are no financial risks involved. Legal exposure is kept to a minimum if those individuals (especially youngsters) who are involved in selling are adequately trained in correct sales tactics and safety considerations. For example, youngsters should not sell in the evenings or travel to strange neighborhoods without an adult. Typically, youngsters should travel in pairs whenever they are selling door-to-door. Finally, the selling process should be low-key and professional. The sponsoring organization would not want to be criticized for employing "hard sell" or offensive tactics.

PERMITS/LICENSES: If solicitors are going to canvas homes, it may be necessary to secure a peddler's permit or hawker's license. Contact your town clerk or other municipal office to find out the requirements in your area.

HINTS: Provide donated prizes to the top salespersons. The ties can be marketed not only for personal use but are great as gift items as well. Parents of youngsters can also become actively involved by taking order forms to work.

Fund raiser #33
Celebrity Hockey Game

POTENTIAL NET INCOME: $4,000

COMPLEXITY/DEGREE OF DIFFICULTY: Moderate

DESCRIPTION: Representatives of a local sport or recreation organization conclude arrangements with a promoter to stage an ice hockey game between N.H.L. Old Stars and the Montreal Old Stars. These two teams travel throughout North America playing benefit games to help promote ice hockey. Net income is generated from ticket sales after payment to the visiting teams. Adults are charged $4 and youngsters between 6 and 18 pay $2 (or whatever the market will bear in your area). Additional profits are generated from the sale of concession items and contributions (sponsorships) from businesses and organizations ($350 each). Paid advertisements can also be solicited for the game program. The game consists of three 20-minute periods. In case of a tie at the end of regulation time, a five-minute sudden death overtime is played. Between the first and second period, donated prizes are awarded to spectators, chosen by chance, who successfully hit the puck (from various distances) into the goal through an obstacle board. Autographs are signed between the second and third period and following the game.

SCHEDULING: The celebrity hockey game may be scheduled on any day, although Friday nights and weekend afternoons and evenings are more popular and hence more profitable.

RESOURCES:

Facilities: Any indoor competitive ice rink will suffice.

Equipment and supplies: Donated prizes, an obstacle board, signs, posters, flyers, tickets, and cash boxes are necessary. Concession equipment and supplies are also required as are food and drink items to be sold to the general public. Printed programs can be created.

Publicity and promotion: Advance publicity involves newspapers, radio and television promotions. Frequently, the media will provide free announcement due to the non-profit nature of the fund raising effort. Highlight in all promotional efforts how the profits from this game will be used within the community. Local businesses and organizations can display signs and posters. Some can even serve as advance ticket sites. Volunteers also make advance ticket sales on an individual basis. And sponsorships are sought by having selected volunteers (centers of influence) approach area businesses and corporations.

Time: This fund raising project can be planned and organized within a week. Making firm arrangements with the touring celebrity hockey teams might take as long as 4-6 weeks. It is essential that the site be reserved and arrangements with the touring teams be confirmed in writing as early as possible, 6-12 months in advance. The selling window to market advance tickets should be kept to a maximum of 3-4 weeks preceding the big game. Allow at least an hour to clean up the facility.

Expenditures: This fund raising project can be initiated with $250, for promotional and publicity efforts and the printing of the game programs. Plan also on spending $250 for concession inventory. The use of the ice hockey site should be obtained free. If not, allocate $500 to rent a facility. Be prepared to spend $50 to make a sign for each sponsor that can be displayed in the arena on game night. The payment for the touring hockey team can be paid for with the profits from the game.

Personnel (Staff/Volunteers): A number of volunteers (30) and staff (2-4) are needed to plan and organize this fund raiser, sell advance tickets, solicit donated prizes and sponsorships from businesses, help publicize and promote the upcoming event, assist in the home event management of the game itself, and serve as members of the set-up and cleanup committee.

RISK MANAGEMENT: The biggest financial risk is the sale of advance and same day tickets. Thus, it is imperative that a significant number of advance tickets be sold to individuals as well as to businesses and organizations. Check that the blanket insurance policy covering the site provides adequate coverage for the sponsoring organization as well as its staff and volunteers.

PERMITS/LICENSES: The sponsors might be required to secure a food permit for the concession stand if such a permit or license has not previously been issued.

HINTS: Schedule the celebrity ice hockey game on a night when there is not a lot of competition for the public's disposable income. Planners would not want to schedule this game in head-to-head competition with other popular youth, high school, collegiate or professional games. Have adults work the ticket booths, handling all ticket and concession monies.

Fund raiser #34
Miniature Golf Tournament

POTENTIAL NET INCOME: $4,000

COMPLEXITY/DEGREE OF DIFFICULTY: Moderate

DESCRIPTION OF PROJECT: An all-day tournament is scheduled at a miniature golf facility where participants (individuals and teams) are eligible for a variety of donated prizes. Refreshments are sold throughout the day and a picnic takes place in early evening. The tournament continues after the picnic with an awards ceremony at the conclusion. Profits are generated from the sale of tickets ($15 profit per person) for golf and the evening picnic. Additional profits result from concession sales. If only 250 individuals take part in the day's activities, the sponsoring organization can easily top $4,000.

SCHEDULING: The golf tournament can be scheduled on any weekend.

RESOURCES:

Facilities: A commercial miniature golf facility is ideal. Or, the organizers can erect their own temporary miniature golf course on a parking lot, playground or vacant lot. The location should be easily accessible by car. If the tournament and related activities extend to evening hours, the area must be lighted.

Equipment and supplies: Golf balls, putters, signs, posters, tickets, picnic tables, chairs, tables, portable gas or charcoal grills, refreshments and cash boxes are all required. If the temporary golf course (18 platforms) must be constructed, wood, paint, glue, screws, and nails as well as a host of tools are necessary. A wide variety of donated prizes are a must. These prizes should all be worth at least $25. Prizes should be awarded both on an individual and team competition in various categories, such as skill level, age, etc.

Publicity and promotion: Publicity and promotional efforts should be aimed both at individuals and at businesses and organizations. Encourage friendly competition among individuals and groups. For example, different real estate offices might field teams to compete against one another. Similarly, different insurance firms could field competitive teams. And representatives of the fire department might take on the officers from the state or local police. Developing this competitive spirit between different businesses and organizations will go a long way toward insuring a large group of participants. Announcements should be placed in area newspapers and penny-savers. The radio and television stations might also mention the upcoming event as part of their public service announcements. Businesses and organizations should be approached to display promotional signs in their offices, to enter the tournament with a team of competitors and to serve as advance ticket sites. Highlight the fact that this is a fund raising effort sponsored by a non-profit community-based organization.

Time: Although this project can be planned and organized in less than a week, it will take considerably longer (3-4 weeks) to confirm all of the arrangements, such as reserving the miniature golf course or constructing a temporary course, selling advance tickets and soliciting gifts and prizes. The promotional or publicity window, including selling of tickets, should not extend beyond 4-5 weeks. Allow 2-3 weeks to build the portable 18-hole miniature golf course. It will take 4-6 hours to erect on site and 3-5 hours to dismantle it.

Expenditures: Prizes should be donated. Similarly, the equipment and supplies should all be secured on a free or loan basis. If a commercial golf facility is utilized, the sponsors should attempt to secure its use gratis or at low cost. If the organizers must construct their own temporary miniature golf course it will be necessary to obtain donated materials and power tools. Out-of-pocket costs might be the promotional and publicity materials as well as food and drink items for the daylong concession operation and the evening picnic. Allocate $350 to kick off this fund raising project.

Personnel (Staff/Volunteers): Volunteers (15-20) and staff (1-2) are needed to sell advance tickets as well as tickets at the gate, to staff the concession stand and the picnic. Some of these helpers should also solicit sponsors to donate a variety of prizes as well as cash. And others will be needed to construct the individual miniature golf holes if a commercial course is not available.

RISK MANAGEMENT: No horseplay at all must be allowed. Golf clubs can become deadly weapons if not used in a safe and intelligent manner. Similarly, golf balls must be putted safely. Assigning volunteer supervisors at strategic locations on the course will insure that safe play is the order of the day. The financial risk is minimal if advance ticket sales are successful and if sufficient sponsors are generous.

PERMITS/LICENSES: A permit might be required for the concession operation. Check with the town clerk or other municipal offices for local requirements.

HINTS: If a portable miniature course must be built, plan a competition to see who can produce the best individual miniature golf hole. Prizes could then be awarded to the groups or organizations for the miniature golf hole judged to be "the best," the "most challenging," the "most original," the "most colorful," the "best decorated," etc. Golfers could fill out ballots to determine the winners. Finally, be sure to make arrangements to securely store the components for each of the golf holes (platforms) for possible use in subsequent years.

Fund raiser #35
Spaghetti Supper

POTENTIAL NET INCOME: $4,000

COMPLEXITY/DEGREE OF DIFFICULTY: Moderate

DESCRIPTION: A dinner consisting of spaghetti, salad, garlic bread, antipasto, and a variety of soft drinks is provided for a most reasonable price. Wine may be sold at an additional cost. Tickets are priced so that the net profit is $4 per dinner. Thus, if 1000 dinners are sold, which is certainly not out of the question in many communities, the sponsoring group would net $4,000. Tickets are sold on an advance basis and at the door.

SCHEDULING: The dinner should be scheduled on a Friday or Saturday afternoon and evening.

RESOURCES:

Facilities: A large indoor area where the food can be prepared and served. A school, recreation site or a local fire hall or VFW facility can all be utilized if adequate space is available. Adequate parking should be available as well. Heavy foot and vehicular traffic nearby is ideal as drop-in customers can more easily be attracted.

Equipment and supplies: Equipment items needed are those items necessary for the preparation and serving of food and drink. Also, poster board and paper are needed for signs. Use of a computer, color printer and graphics software aids in creating eye-catching flyers, posters and signs. Consumable items include spaghetti, salad, garlic bread, antipasto, and a variety of soft drinks. A cash box with $150 in change, a receipt book and a record book are also needed.

Publicity and promotion: The key to success is advance publicity and promotion. Announcements in the area news media are a must. Mention of the Spaghetti Supper should be included within the sponsoring organization's own printed materials, announcements at athletic contests or recreational activities. Posters should be displayed in area businesses and flyers should be distributed throughout the community at houses as well as placed on vehicles at area malls and shopping centers. Advertising on the day of the event includes signs outside the facility as well as flyers given to passersby. Be sure that ALL the publicity includes how the money raised will be spent within the community.

Time: The Spaghetti Supper can be held from 2 p.m.-9 p.m. The planning period can be short, 1 or 2 weeks. However, promotional efforts are more involved and can take up to 4-5 weeks. Volunteers are staggered in their work assignments on the day of the event so that no one works more than 3-4 hours at a crack. Plan on spending 3-4 hours on cleanup activities.

Expenditures: Hopefully, the promoters will be able to secure many of the food and drink items as well as paper products on a donated basis or, at least, on a reduced cost basis. Start-up costs should not exceed $500 for all items, including food, drink, marketing and publicity.

Personnel (Staff/Volunteers): This can be a very labor intensive fund raiser. Fifteen to 25 volunteers are needed at any one time, to help prepare the food, to serve the customers and to continually provide cleanup for the dining area. Helpers may be needed in the parking area to direct traffic. Volunteers and staff are also involved in selling advance tickets, preparing and distributing flyers and signs and helping promote the dinner. Adult volunteers must be assigned to collect money or tickets at the door.

RISK MANAGEMENT: Sponsors should be especially careful that all health regulations are followed in terms of storage, preparation and serving of food. Nothing is worse for the fund raising event itself and for the sponsoring entity than having a scandal such as food poisoning taint the event. Keep financial risks minimal by being able to return all unopened, unused food and drink containers to the wholesaler following the event.

PERMITS/LICENSES: Local municipal officials should be queried to determine if a specific permit needs to be secured for this food event. In many communities no special license need be obtained, especially if the event is held in the sponsoring organization's own facility. This does not, however, diminish the need to abide by all health, safety, and food regulations. If wine or beer is to be served during the dinner a special permit (issued either locally or at the state level) may be required. Finally, some communities have regulations that prohibit or regulate the distribution of flyers to individual homes or at shopping areas. Check with the local town clerk or municipal offices to see whether any such rules are applicable in your community.

HINTS: In today's high tech world, many fund raising organizations have no difficulty in borrowing or receiving permission to use computers, etc., from their supporters or from local businesses. Promoters should not forget about "take-out" orders (or even delivery service) as this can provide a significant portion of the total profit, and advertisements and promotional activities should highlight this service.

Fund raiser #36
Gift Box for the Boss

POTENTIAL NET INCOME: $4,300

COMPLEXITY/DEGREE OF DIFFICULTY: Low

DESCRIPTION: Attractive gift boxes are stuffed with a variety of gift items and then sold to employees as appreciation gifts for their bosses on National Bosses' (Appreciation) Day (October 16th). The individual gift boxes can contain any number of items, such as a congratulatory card, fresh and preserved food, a tie, a coffee mug, candy, a ticket to an athletic or theater event, gift certificates, etc. If five or more gift boxes are purchased by employees at a single business or organization the gift boxes are delivered at no additional cost. Otherwise, they must be picked up by the purchasers on a specific date. The price of the gift packages is set so as to create a profit of at least $15 per box, exclusive of publicity and promotional expenses. Generally speaking, the selling price is determined by what the market will bear. The money is collected when the order is taken. If only 300 gift boxes are sold the net profit approaches $4,500.

SCHEDULING: This fund raising project centers around 5-7 weeks prior to the National Bosses' Day, October 16th.

RESOURCES:

Facilities: A facility must be secured where the gift items can be stored until they are packed into the boxes. They must then be stored until they are either picked up or delivered as arranged. Also, a convenient site must be available for purchasers to pick up the gift boxes on the appointed day during specific hours.

Equipment and supplies: Individual boxes as well as cards, food, candy, free tickets, gift certificates, etc., must be secured. Signs, posters, order forms and receipt books are also required.

Publicity and promotion: Information about this fund raiser needs to be disseminated throughout the community through announcements in area news papers, including the local penny-savers. Even radio and television stations might give this project a plug as part of their Public Service Announcements (PSAs). Highlight the fact that the sponsoring group is a non-profit organization and publicize how the proceeds from this fund raiser will be put to good use within the community. Local businesses and organizations should be asked to display signs and posters promoting and publicizing the gift boxes. Some businesses can even serve as order takers.

Time: The appreciation day gift box fund raising project can be planned and organized within 1 or 2 weeks. However, allow an additional 3-4 weeks to solicit and collect the individual gifts for the boxes. The publicity and selling window should be kept to 4-5 weeks, at a maximum. The gift boxes not delivered should be made available for pick-up the preceding weekend before the event, from 1 p.m. to 4:30 p.m. Those boxes that are to be delivered should be given to the individual purchasers on the day or two prior to this date.

Expenditures: Allocate $200 for promotional and publicity efforts (including the personalized "greeting card" for each box). All of the gift items in each box are donated. The cost of the individual boxes will be around 50 cents if they cannot be donated.

Personnel (Staff/Volunteers): The organizers will need volunteers (30-33) and staff (1-2) to assist with (1) collecting orders and actual selling of the gift packages to employees, (2) the solicitation and collection of gift items, (3) the storage of the items, (4) the packing of the gift items within each container, (5) the distribution of boxes on collection day, and (6) delivery of those boxes when five or more have been ordered from the same location.

RISK MANAGEMENT: There is no financial risk since the money is collected when the order is taken. Likewise, the legal liability risk is negligible as long as the food items are of quality and all health rules and regulations regarding to storage and wrapping, etc., are strictly followed. Gifts should be truly gifts, no "free" house appraisals by Realtors and no "free" insurance evaluations.

PERMITS/LICENSES: Since there is no door-to-door selling involved, there is no need for special permits or licenses.

HINTS: Set up a telephone "hot line" where orders may be placed and publicize where orders and checks may be mailed. The individual gifts can be obtained from a variety of sources, including area colleges and universities (free tickets to athletic, art and theater events), professional teams (free event tickets), area farm markets (food items such as jams, dried flowers, baked goods, etc.), grocery stores (candy, food and drink items), printers (congratulatory cards), florists (flowers and cards), bakeries (fresh breads), department stores (gift certificates), movie theaters (free tickets), professional car wash (free washes), etc. It is not absolutely necessary that each box contain identical items. In fact, there is an advantage to variety when more than one gift box is ordered by employees at the same business.

Fund raiser #37
Custom Birdhouse Auction

POTENTIAL NET INCOME: $4,500

COMPLEXITY/DEGREE OF DIFFICULTY: Moderate

DESCRIPTION: Artfully crafted birdhouses, some replicas of famous buildings such as the White House, the Capitol building, etc., are built by volunteer craft persons, and beautifully painted and decorated. These birdhouses are auctioned off following a semi-formal dinner party. The tables and room decorations reflect the theme of birds. There are even bird cages with live birds positioned throughout the room. Both the cages and birds are also auctioned off during the evening's festivities. Donated door prizes are given away periodically during the dinner and auction. Only advance dinner tickets are sold and are priced so that the organizing group will realize a $15 net profit per person. Corporate and business sponsorships are secured to help defray expenses.

SCHEDULING: The dinner and auction can be scheduled for any Friday or Saturday evening.

RESOURCES:

Facilities: A dining establishment or party house capable of serving 250-300 persons is needed. Close and safe parking is a must.

Equipment and supplies: 50-75 birdhouses, bird cages and birds, flyers, posters, markers, lists of items to be auctioned, theme oriented decorations, public address system, donated door prizes, tables for the bird cages, invitations and tickets are all required.

Publicity and promotion: Extensive publicity surrounding this dinner and auction is necessary. Local newspapers and penny-savers should include blurbs about the fund raiser. The area radio and television stations might also provide important publicity and promotion for this event as part of their Public Service Announcements (PSAs). Announcements can be made over the public address systems at other sport and recreation activities. Special printed invitations sent to prospective patrons, important people, and "heavy hitters" can be most effective in encouraging individual and corporate participation. Corporate sponsorship of tables is encouraged by influential members of the community who happen to also be fans, supporters or members of the booster group.

Time: Secure a suitable site at least six months in advance. Ticket reservations and money must be in by a specific deadline, usually two weeks prior to the dinner. Start the promotional and publicity campaign at least 6 weeks before the dinner. Plan on spending 3 hours to set up the facility with appropriate decorations. Cleanup will involve at least an hour.

Expenditures: Initial seed money will run as high as $500 and includes a refundable deposit for the facility and publicity costs. The bird- houses are donated as are the door prizes, bird cages and live birds. Don't be bashful in attempting to secure donated or loaned items. The organizers should never pay full price for anything, not even the use of the site, due to the non-profit nature of the sponsoring group and the worthy cause for which the event is being held. Specify how the profits will be put to good use.

Personnel (Staff/Volunteers): A relatively small group of dedicated volunteers (15-20) and staff (2-4) are needed to plan, organize and implement this dinner/auction. These helpers are involved in ironing out all of the details of the event, securing sponsors, donations, prizes, etc. The birdhouses are constructed and decorated by a small number (3-7) of skilled individuals. A greater number of volunteers and boosters (30-45) are needed to purchase tickets themselves and to help sell the tickets within the community, usually face-to-face.

RISK MANAGEMENT: The greatest risk involves the financial exposure associated with the selling of tickets. It is imperative that the ticket sales be strongly promoted by volunteers and staff members assigned to this task. Thus, the organizers need to establish a break-even point in terms of the number of tickets that must be sold to not lose money. If that number of tickets is not sold by at least three weeks prior to the date, the dinner/auction should be called off. If at a restaurant or party house, the legal liability associated with the serving of food and drink is minimal.

PERMITS/LICENSES: No special permits or licenses are required if the event is held at a restaurant or party house.

HINTS: Negotiate a deadline prior to which the dinner arrangements may be cancelled with the restaurant or party house if insufficient tickets are sold. Thus, a refundable deposit may be returned if the event is called off prior to that date.

Fund raiser #38
Dinner Dance

POTENTIAL NET INCOME: $4,500

COMPLEXITY/DEGREE OF DIFFICULTY: Moderate.

DESCRIPTION: A sit-down or buffet style dinner followed by a dance for a minimum of 100 couples comprises this fund raiser. Advance tickets are sold for $75 per couple—or whatever the market will bear.

SCHEDULING: A Friday or Saturday evening is ideal. The dance can be scheduled at any time of the year.

RESOURCES:

Facilities: If the entire affair can be held in the school or recreation facility the savings can be significant, although something might be lacking in terms of atmosphere. The dinner dance could also be scheduled in a restaurant, if a large enough dance floor is available. If a very large crowd (150-200 couples) is expected, even a party house or golf club party room could be booked.

Equipment and supplies: If the event is held in a commercial establishment, all of the equipment and supplies as well as the set-up and preparation of the meals will be included in the cost of the rental agreement. If special decorations are necessary, these can be purchased or secured on a loan or donated basis.

Publicity and promotion: Since the ultimate success depends upon the number of advance tickets sold, it is imperative that effective marketing, publicity and promotional efforts be undertaken. Displays and posters strategically located in area businesses coupled with announcements in newspapers and free pennysavers as well as periodic public service announcements (PSAs) by local radio and television stations will help make a large segment of the community aware of this special fund raiser. Target the entire community as ticket buyers. Emphasize the fun aspect of the event, but don't neglect to also highlight the merit of the fund raising project.

Time: The dinner dance is scheduled to run from 7 p.m. until midnight or even 1 a.m. The dinner portion (from soup to nuts) typically takes about 90 minutes with the remainder of the evening devoted to dancing. Planning for this event will take four weeks. Anticipate another month for promoting, marketing and selling the tickets. The selling window should be kept relatively short as most of the tickets that can be sold will be sold during this time period.

Expenditures: The cost of the meals (which includes use of the facility) will vary depending upon what is served and the type of facility. However, a figure of $25 per couple is reasonable. Always inquire about a price break due to the non-profit nature of your organization and the worthiness of the fund raising project. The other major costs involve obtaining an excellent band or securing the services of a disc-jockey (with appropriate records or tapes) as well as marketing, promotional, music and decorating expenses. Plan on spending another $500.

Personnel (Staff/Volunteers): Volunteers and sport or recreation staff members (30-35) are needed to distribute, sell and collect tickets as well as to distribute advertising flyers and posters within the community. Another five volunteers will be needed on the evening of the dance for last-minute details and to thank those attending.

RISK MANAGEMENT: The greatest risk involved is not selling sufficient tickets to cover expenses. To prevent this catastrophe establish a cut-off date by which a final decision will be made whether or not to continue with plans. And, of course, final commitment to the restaurant or party house and the bank or DJ may be cancelled as of this arbitrary cut-off date.

PERMITS/LICENSES: None.

HINTS: There are an infinite number of different types of dinner dances: a formal affair, a western square dance, a sock-hop, a costume dance, etc. Even so-called movie themes, such as *South Pacific, Gone With the Wind, The Godfather,* and others, can be used or try holiday themes such as Christmas, Halloween, New Year's Eve, Valentine's Day, etc. If successful, the dinner dance can become an annual affair.

Fund raiser #39
Discount "Credit" Cards

POTENTIAL NET INCOME: $4,500

COMPLEXITY/DEGREE OF DIFFICULTY: Moderate

DESCRIPTION: Small plastic cards, each the size of a credit card, are sold for $5 apiece, generating a $4 profit for each card sold. The cards contain printed discounts for goods and/or services from 18 local businesses such as restaurants, sporting goods stores, gas stations, pizza parlors, etc. The discounts are good for any number of times for a period of one calendar year. Purchasers need only present their card to the merchant in order to obtain the stated discount. If each of 35 volunteers sell 40 cards the net profit is $4,500.

SCHEDULING: This fund raiser can be initiated at any time of the year. Some organizers have scheduled the selling window to coincide with the Christmas holidays, marketing the cards as stocking stuffers.

RESOURCES:

Facilities: None.

Equipment and supplies: A supply of discount cards must be purchased. Signs and posters are needed to help publicize and promote the activity.

Publicity and promotion: Area businesses and organizations can display signs and posters advertising the availability of the discount cards. Some businesses can even sell the cards. Area newspapers and pennysavers can provide much needed publicity. The local radio and television stations might also include this fund raising effort as part of their public service announcements (PSAs). Don't forget to use the PA system at other events organized by the sponsoring group to promote the purchase of cards. The best and most effective publicity activity is the actual selling of the cards to individuals on a person-to-person basis. Parents can even take cards to work and attempt to sell them.

Time: This fund raising project can be planned and organized within a week. Securing 18 businesses to agree to participate by offering worthwhile discounts over a year's time might take 4-8 weeks. It will take approximately 2-4 weeks to order and receive the plastic cards, printed on both sides, and containing the appropriate logo of the organizing group as well as the 18 different discounts from the area businesses. After the cards have been received, the selling window should not extend beyond 3-4 weeks.

Expenditures: If 1,400 cards are ordered, the cost to have them printed will be $1,400. Allocate another $100 for promotional and publicity expenses and the organizers will have an initial down-side risk of $1,500.

Personnel (Staff/Volunteers): 35 volunteers and staff are needed to sell the cards and help in the promotional activity. Other helpers (10-15) are needed to solicit the various discounts and donated prizes from businesses.

RISK MANAGEMENT: Be sure the expiration date for the discounts is printed plainly on the cards. If the expiration date is July 1, 1999, the selling window should conclude prior to June 30, 1998, to insure that all purchasers would have a full 12-months to take advantage of the multiple discounts. There is a sizeable financial risk to be undertaken by the sponsors of this fund raiser in that $1,400 will need to be spent prior to any income. Organizers need to carefully evaluate how many discount cards can realistically be marketed within the area in the allocated time period. It is essential that a low-key approach be used. A hard sell approach can only create negative publicity as well as a negative image for the sponsors and their organization. Be sure that the businesses offering the discounts understand that the discounts may be taken advantage of any number of times during the 12-month period. A signed agreement, specifically outlining the discount, between the individual merchant and the sponsoring organization should prevent any misunderstandings. Also, the discounts must really be meaningful, such as one meal free when an identical meal is purchased at a restaurant. Or $2 off at the local professional car wash or off any haircut at a local barbershop or beauty salon. No free house appraisals or insurance evaluations should be part of this discount card.

PERMITS/LICENSES: If the cards are to be sold door-to-door, some communities require a peddler's permit or hawker's license. Check with the town clerk or bureau of licenses.

HINTS: Highlight the fact that this is a fund raising effort by a local, non-profit organization. Publicize how the money will be put to use within the community. Donated prizes may be given to the top sellers. If there are cards left over at the conclusion of the selling window, plan a last minute sales effort for a period of 3-4 days in which the remaining cards are distributed to the top sellers. Any remaining unsold cards can be used as prizes to be given away throughout the year as part of other promotional activities.

Fund raiser #40
St. Valentine's Day Dinner Dance

POTENTIAL NET INCOME: $5,200

COMPLEXITY/DEGREE OF DIFFICULTY: Moderate

DESCRIPTION: The dinner can consist of a buffet followed by dancing. The type of music is left entirely up to the organizers of the event and should be selected by what type of music will attract the greatest number of people. Tickets are sold for $75 per couple. If the costs per couple (including meals, usage of the facility, band, and promotions) average around $35, the potential profit for the evening, if 130 couples attend, is $5,200.

SCHEDULING: St. Valentine's Day (February 14th) falls on different days of the week. The fund raising dance could be held on the Friday or Saturday evening following the day or on the 14th itself.

RESOURCES:

Facilities: A suitable facility which has room for both dining and dancing for approximately 100-250 couples. A professional party house might be rented or a restaurant may be booked. The sponsoring organization's own site may be used but only if the appropriate cooking facilities, equipment and supplies are adequate and if the site meets the requirements in terms of indoor space, parking and atmosphere.

Equipment and supplies: The decorations for the evening's festivities should revolve around the theme and colors (red & white) of the holiday. Appropriate party favors and centerpieces could be provided for each of the tables. Posters, flyers and announcements must also be secured.

Publicity and promotion: Advance tickets must be readily available. Announcements in the area media are essential, including pennysavers. Don't forget to display promotional posters and flyers at various businesses. Selected businesses can also sell tickets. Mention of the dance at different athletic or recreational events is also recommended. Development of a master list of potential ticket purchasers (donors) will facilitate the sponsoring group's ability to pinpoint those individuals and groups most likely to support the recreation or sport entity by buying a ticket(s).

Time: The dinner begins at 6:30 p.m. with dancing at around 8 p.m. till 1 a.m. Planning for this event will take up to two weeks. Reserve at least 3-4 weeks for the actual marketing, promoting and selling of the tickets.

Expenditures: Payment for decorations, flyers, posters, publicity, the band; and, of course, for the meals (and site rental, if any) must be paid for from the gross profits of the dinner dance—unless obtained on a donated or reduced cost basis. Plan on spending $200 in seed money to get this project off the ground. Don't neglect to solicit donations or seek reduced prices for everything that must be purchased for the dance.

Personnel (Staff/Volunteers): Staff (2-3) and volunteers (20-25) form the foundation of the sales force for the tickets. These same individuals can actively be involved in the planning and set-up of the facility in terms of decorations, seat assignments, etc.

RISK MANAGEMENT: The danger in this type of fund raiser is what you do if no one shows up. This nightmare must be prevented at all costs both to protect the pocketbook of the sponsoring group and its reputation and credibility. One way to solve this problem is to pre-sell tickets to members, "friends," or boosters of the sponsoring sport or recreation organization thus giving the planning group an idea of the number to expect. Another tactic is to determine a cut-off date by which a specific number of tickets must be sold (thus generating a profit) in order for the dinner dance to actually take place. A third way to address the danger of insufficient participation is to have some potential donor "insure" the event by agreeing to make up the difference between the actual cost of the event and the income generated, if a profit is not realized through ticket sales.

PERMITS/LICENSES: If the dinner dance is held in a restaurant or party House, there is no need for special permits or licenses.

HINTS: During the evening officers of the sponsoring organization should take time to individually thank all of those in attendance. Additionally, those attending should be informed as to how much money has been raised and how the funds will be used. Once this event has been recognized as a success both by the organizers and those who attended, plans can be instituted to make this an annual event. It will be decidedly easier the second time around because the attendees should want to take part, and those who worked on the project will have had experience in implementing this type of event and will be able, hopefully, to make it even more enjoyable and successful in the future.

Fund raising projects to generate between $5,000 and $10,000

4

Chapter 4

Fund raising projects to generate between $5,000 and $10,000

Fund raiser #41
Couch Potato Contest

POTENTIAL NET INCOME: $5,500 annually

COMPLEXITY/DEGREE OF DIFFICULTY: Low

DESCRIPTION: Raffle tickets may be purchased for $1 apiece or 10 for $5. Winners are able to be couch potatoes at an indoor sports activity by sitting court-side on a couch, with two friends. At the beginning of the game, the winner and the two guests are treated to large pizzas, a 12-pack of soda, and dessert. The couch potatoes sit back and enjoy the contest and their refreshments just as if they were at home in front of their TVs. Raffle tickets may be purchased for $1 apiece or 10 for $5. This fund raising project can be held at every home basketball game as well as other indoor athletic contests. With an average take of only $200 per contest, the sponsoring group can reap over $6,000 if the contest is held at 30 home events.

SCHEDULING: This contest can be held whenever there is an appropriate inside athletic contest scheduled.

RESOURCES:

Facilities: The couch potato fund raiser can take place at almost any indoor athletic competition such as basketball, wrestling, volleyball, etc. A nearby storage room is needed for the couch between games. The room needs to be close to the playing court to facilitate moving it.

Equipment and supplies: A couch (preferably one that can be discarded after the season), signs, posters, tickets, a "fish" bowl from which the winning ticket is drawn.

Publicity and supplies: The PA system should periodically announce the couch potato raffle. Also, promote the ongoing fund raising effort by utilizing the PA system during the contest to point out the winner(s) enjoying the contest from their court side perch. Signs should be prominently displayed alongside the ticket booth and inside the facility explaining the raffle. Be sure to publicize how the profits from the yearlong fund raising project will be used to benefit the sport program. Even the printed programs should include a short blurb publicizing the raffle. Area merchants might be asked to display signs or posters. Due to its unique nature, the fund raiser should be covered by area news media, both print and electronic.

Time: This fund raiser can be planned and organized in a matter of days. Allow some time prior to each contest to move the couch to the prearranged spot. Similarly, plan on spending 5-10 minutes putting the couch away in storage until the next contest.

Expenditures: Since the prizes (pizza, soda and dessert) awarded to the winner(s) are donated from area businesses, there are few costs to with this project. Even the used couch should be donated. Plan on spending less than $50 (signs, posters and tickets) to kick off the couch potato contest.

Personnel (Staff/Volunteers): A small number of volunteers (5-7) and staff (1-2) are needed to plan the event, to secure the food items to be given to the winners, to sell the raffle tickets, to announce the winner(s) and to move the couch to the prearranged site next to the playing court.

RISK MANAGEMENT: There is no financial risk associated with this fund raising effort. To minimize accidents, be sure that the couch is situated in a safe place near the athletic competition. You would not want the winners to be run over by athletes before, during or after the game.

PERMITS/LICENSES: Check with the town clerk or other municipal offices to see whether a gambling permit is required to conduct the raffle.

HINTS: Almost any athletic contest, even outdoors, can sponsor a couch potato contest. However, in this event, be prepared for inclement weather and provide for a tent to cover the winner(s). If this contest is held in connection with a swimming and diving event, be prepared for the couch to suffer permanent damage due to the humidity in the facility. This same fund raising concept can also be utilized by recreation organizations at any number of different events at which tickets are sold. This project is essentially a no-brainer—but is extremely popular and profitable. Be sure adults sell the tickets and account for the money. Similarly, an adult should be responsible for pulling the winning ticket from the "fish" bowl. The contest must be conducted with integrity. For each home contest, publicly thank—via PA announcements as well as strategically located signs (perhaps on the back of the couch itself)—those individuals and/or businesses who contributed (for example, by donating the food and drink items) to the couch potato contest.

Fund raiser #42
Hole-in-One Contest

POTENTIAL NET INCOME: $5,500

COMPLEXITY/DEGREE OF DIFFICULTY: Low

DESCRIPTION: Chances to win $10,000 by hitting a hole-in-one on one or more designated par-three golf holes are sold for $5 to the general public. Numerous donated prizes are also given away each day for those golfers who come close.

SCHEDULING: This fund raiser may be scheduled whenever weather permits. In most parts of the country, almost anytime during the summer is acceptable. This contest lasts 10 days to two weeks, and may be especially profitable if it is held in conjunction with one or more professional or amateur golf tournaments in the area.

RESOURCES:

Facilities: One or more par-three golf holes. Or, a hole may be constructed solely for this particular fund raising event on an already existing athletic or recreation field.

Equipment and supplies: Posters, signs, flyers, golf clubs, specially marked balls, entry forms, cash boxes and receipt/record books are needed. Donated prizes should also be made available for those golfers who come close to making the hole-in-one.

Publicity and supplies: The community at large is made aware of this fund raising project through publicity announcements in local newspapers and penny-savers. The local radio and television stations can also provide free publicity as part of their Public Service Announcements (PSAs). Businesses and organizations should display signs or posters. Flyers can also be placed on the windshields of vehicles parked at area malls or shopping centers. Highly visible signs should be placed at the site of the contest. In the promotional efforts, highlight the fact that this is a fund raising effort sponsored by a local non-profit organization for a worthy cause, that the profits will be put to good use in the community.

Time: This simple project can be planned and organized within a week. Securing an insurance company to underwrite the policy to pay off the $10,000 in event of a successful hole-in-one might take 3-4 weeks.

Expenditures: This fund raiser can be kicked off for around $150 for promotional efforts and another $500 for the special risk insurance policy.

Personnel (Staff/Volunteers): Volunteers (25-30) and staff (1-2) must be available to supervise contestants attempting to make the hole-in-one. These helpers should be scheduled on a rotating basis in pairs to collect the money and to insure that all of the rules are obeyed. Some of these volunteers are also needed to gather donated prizes (goods and services).

RISK MANAGEMENT: The greatest financial risk is that someone might actually hit a hole-in-one and be entitled to the $10,000 prize. To protect the sponsoring organization from this financial obligation, an insurance policy must be secured to cover the payout should someone be successful. The insurance company will insist upon some very specific guidelines and rules to govern the contest. For example, there must be present designated individuals overseeing each attempt to insure honesty. The minimum length between the pin and the hole will most certainly be specified. Even the layout of the "hole" itself must be approved in advance by the insurance company representative. There could be other rules and stipulations as well, for example, no professional golfers may participate, etc. Seek permission from shopping center managers before distributing promotional flyers on parked vehicles in their parking lots.

PERMITS/LICENSES: Since this is a game of chance, it may be necessary to secure permission or a license form the local or state gaming board.

HINTS: Be prepared to meet the rigorous requirements that may be stipulated by the insurance company. Some organizers have created a hole-in-one facility right on their own property. This is especially effective if the site is near a heavily traveled intersection.

Fund raising #43
Spell-a-Thon

POTENTIAL NET INCOME: $5,500

COMPLEXITY/DEGREE OF DIFFICULTY: Low

DESCRIPTION OF PROJECT: Pledges are solicited based on the number of words to be correctly spelled by youngsters on either a single or multiple spelling tests. The spell-a-thon involves the youngsters being given up to 100 words which they must successfully spell (write). The pledges are obtained by the youngsters involved; they solicit pledges from family and friends. This spelling test can be held in connection with a sporting event or recreation activity or as a stand-alone event.

SCHEDULING: The spell-a-thon may be scheduled at any time of the year. The event can be held on a Saturday or Sunday afternoon or on Friday evening.

RESOURCES:

Facilities: The spell-a-thon can take place in almost any type of indoor facility. The contest can be in a classroom, a gymnasium or any large room which will accommodate the children. If an audience is involved there must be adequate room for these spectators to sit. Adequate parking is necessary.

Equipment and supplies: Pencils, paper, scoring pads, blackboard(s), tables, chairs, pledge forms, PA system, magic markers, posters and signs are all necessary.

Publicity and supplies: Announcements should be sent to area newspapers, including the pennysavers. Local radio and television stations might help publicize this fund raiser as part of their public service announcements. Be sure to highlight the educational nature of this contest as well as the non-profit nature of the sponsoring organization and the worthy nature of the fund raising project itself, i.e., how the money will be put to use within the community. Signs and posters should be displayed in local businesses.

Time: The fund raising project can be planned and organized within a week or two. Reserve the site for the spell-a-thon as early as possible. Schedule at least one hour session to train the youngsters how to safely and efficiently solicit pledges. Keep the actual time period for pledges to no more than 3-4 weeks. The actual spell-a-thon can be completed on a single date or may be spread over several days (events). Allow a weekend for pledges to be collected.

Expenditures: This fund raiser can be initiated with less than $100 in expenditures. The organizers should attempt to solicit as many items as possible (posters, signs, magic markers, pledge forms, etc.) on a donated or greatly reduced basis thereby limiting the amount of cash necessary.

Personnel (Staff/Volunteers): The key to this fund raising project is having sufficient numbers of youngsters (50) and adults (10) soliciting pledges. A colorful and entertaining master of ceremonies can make the spell-a-thon an entertaining event. Additional volunteers (5) and staff (1-2) are needed to plan and follow through with details.

RISK MANAGEMENT: Youngsters should reveal to potential donors that their contributions will not exceed a specific dollar amount. That is, a prospective donor making a 25-cent pledge should be apprised that there is the potential for a total contribution of $25 if the youngster spells all 100 words correctly. There should never be any surprises for the donors in terms of how much they have actually committed themselves to as a result of their pledge. Financial risks are minimal due to the nature of this project. However, there is always the potential for legal liability exposure in light of the pledge solicitation process itself. To reduce the likelihood of youngsters being injured while seeking pledged it is important to have a training session for these young people. They need to be instructed in the safety aspects of soliciting pledges (walking in pairs, soliciting in neighborhoods where they are known and not seeking pledges in the evenings without an adult.)

PERMITS/LICENSES: Some communities require a peddler's license or hawker's permit if any type of fund raising effort is to be made door-to-door. Check with the town clerk or the local bureau of licensing.

HINTS: Potential contributors can include anyone in the community although those who have some connection to the sponsoring organization and/or the youngsters involved in the fund raiser are most likely to contribute. Anticipate that there will be approximately 10%-15% "leakage" between the amount of money pledged and the actual dollars collected. Instead of planning the spell-a-thon as a stand-alone event, the organizers might want to consider including a concession stand or adding a bake sale to increase profits.

Fund raiser #44
Adopt/Sponsor An Athlete

POTENTIAL NET INCOME: $6,000

COMPLEXITY/DEGREE OF DIFFICULTY: Low

DESCRIPTION: Individuals, businesses and organizations are approached to "adopt" an athlete by sponsoring an individual youngster for a special activity, such as a trip to a distant sport camp, tournament or competition. Such sponsorships can include the total amount of what it would cost to send the athlete or any part of the costs. In the latter case, multiple sponsors may be solicited to help pay for an individual athlete. In an instance where the cost per youngster is $400, a team consisting of 15 youngsters would need to generate $6,000 in contributions (via sponsors).

SCHEDULING: This fund raising solicitation may be conducted at any time of the year.

RESOURCES:

Facilities: No special facilities are needed.

Equipment and supplies: Signs and posters need to be created for publicity purposes. An attractive flyer explaining the purpose of the solicitation should also be created. And pledge sheets should be printed to aid in recordkeeping.

Publicity and supplies: This entire fund raising solicitation campaign is promoted as "adopt an athlete" program. A one-page, typed outline (flyer) explaining the purpose of the fund raising request and providing background information about the sport organization itself should be made available to and left with potential sponsors, who can be approached on the basis of "adopting" an individual youngster for the upcoming trip. Some youngsters might have more than one sponsor, each of whom contributes part of the total cost. Signs and posters publicizing the proposed trip (or camp participation) and the upcoming solicitation should be displayed in various businesses and organizations. Newspapers and radio stations should be sent news releases explaining the purpose of the solicitation, highlighting the worthy nature of the fund raising.

Time: This fund raising project can be planned and organized within two weeks. Allow 4-5 weeks for the actual solicitation of pledges and another 2-3 days for the collection of the contributions. It is suggested that the solicitation of sponsors be initiated well in advance of the proposed sport trip in case there are difficulties in obtaining sufficient contributions.

Expenditures: Less than $100 need be spent for publicity and promotional supplies. Recognition plaques or trophies to be given to each of the major contributing sponsors will cost another $150.

Personnel (Staff/Volunteers): Youngsters (15), adult volunteers (30) and staff (1-2) can all play a big part in the solicitation process.

RISK MANAGEMENT: There are no financial risks or unusual legal liability dangers inherent in this type of fund raising effort.

PERMITS/LICENSES: None.

HINTS: If youngsters are going to meet with potential contributors, take time to train them in how to present their request for pledges. Frequently, the person-to-person approach is the most effective way to generate the needed monies. It is better to initially approach affluent individuals in an effort to secure one sponsor per athlete. Depending upon the amount that needs to be raised for each youngster, it is more efficient, and frequently more effective, to approach 15-20 heavy hitters asking each for the total amount to sponsor one youngster than to attempt to solicit numerous $5, $10 and $15 contributions. Be sure to have the individual youngsters write a personal "thank-you" note to their sponsor(s) before the individual leaves on the trip. During the time the athlete is away, another written communication (letter and/or post card) should be sent to the sponsor(s) by each youngster. And, following the conclusion of the experience, each sponsor should receive some type of memento from the sport organization itself (trophy, plaque and/or commendation letter—depending upon how much each individual sponsor contributed) as an expression of thanks and appreciation from the youngster and the organization. It is important to treat sponsors in a professional manner so that in the future they as well as others might be inclined to help again.

Fund raiser #45
Alumni(ae) Athletic Cookout

POTENTIAL NET INCOME: $6,000

COMPLEXITY/DEGREE OF DIFFICULTY: High

DESCRIPTION: Former athletes, coaches, managers and administrators are invited back to school to participate in a variety of sport and recreational contests preceding and following an outdoor noon cookout. These former participants team up with and against each other as well as members from the community. The athletic contests can involve almost any sport: flag football, basketball, softball, tennis, table tennis, swimming, etc. A "donation" of $35 is sought from participants as well as spectators, both alumni and members of the general public. There should be no hesitation in having even the alumni(ae) pay the admission fee if everyone realizes that this is a fund raising effort. If a mere 200 individuals are involved, the net profit can easily reach $6,000. If 300 people pay to take part, the profit is $10,500.

SCHEDULING: This fund raising project is scheduled on a Saturday when excellent weather is expected.

RESOURCES:

Facilities: Outdoor as well as indoor athletic facilities are required. In case of inclement weather all of the athletic competitions are to be held indoors as well as the food activities.

Equipment and supplies: Organizers need to provide all appropriate sport equipment and supplies to facilitate the friendly competition. Donated trophies, ribbons and other types of prizes (gift certificates, athletic equipment, etc.) must also be available. A cash box, tickets, tables, chairs, portable gas and/or charcoal grills as well as an outdoor PA system are a must. Additional cooking equipment can be borrowed and other supplies (paper napkins, cups and plates and plastic utensils) can be donated. Of course, food and drink also should be donated from sponsors and solicited well in advance. Signs, posters, stationery and stamps are all required to promote the event.

Publicity and supplies: Special announcements are mailed out to the sport alumni(ae). Additionally, announcements in the area news media including the penny-savers will provide much-needed publicity. Local radio and television stations might provide gratis publicity as part of their public service announcements. If the organizing group has a periodic newsletter, mention of this fund raiser should be prominently highlighted in several issues. Local businesses can display signs and posters. Don't forget to highlight the fund raising aspect.

Time: The fund raiser can be planned and organized in two or three weeks. However, the advance publicity and invitations should be sent out some 2-4 months in advance. And the site/facility reservations must be confirmed in writing before any invitations are sent out or publicity released. Plan on spending 2-3 hours to prepare the facility as well as an hour or two to clean up. The day's activities begin around 9 or 10 a.m. and will conclude around 5 or 6 p.m.

Expenditures: If corporate or business sponsors are obtained, most if not all of the costs of this fund raising project can be covered. However, allocate at least $250 to kick off the all-day event.

Personnel (Staff/Volunteers): Volunteers (30-35) and staff (1-2) are needed to plan and implement this project.

RISK MANAGEMENT: Legal liability exposure can be reduced if great care is taken in the storage, preparation and dispensing of food and drink items. The financial risk is negated with successful solicitation of sponsors that pay for the fund raising costs.

PERMITS/LICENSES: Anytime there is food sold, organizers should check with the health department or town clerk to see if a license/permit is necessary.

HINTS: The key to the success of this project rests in securing corporate sponsors that contribute cash as well as tangible gifts and the loan of equipment items. If the costs of conducting the day-long event can be thus covered, all income generated results in pure profit.

Fund raiser #46
Day Sport Camp

POTENTIAL NET INCOME: $6,000 per week

COMPLEXITY/DEGREE OF DIFFICULTY: High

DESCRIPTION: The tuition for the five-day camp in a specific sport ranges between $80-$90 for youngsters in 4th grade through high school. Concessions and sales of souvenir merchandise can become sizeable sources of additional profits. The camp may be co-ed or single sex.

SCHEDULING: The activities are scheduled to begin on Monday morning at 9 a.m. and run each day until 5 p.m. The camp concludes at the end of the week, on Friday. The activities are scheduled so that the athletes have breakfast and dinner at home and for lunch can either bring their own or purchase food and drinks from the concession stand. Other sport and recreational activities can be periodically scheduled during the week to maintain the interest and enthusiasm of the youngsters.

RESOURCES:

Facilities: A suitable sport facility with sufficient indoor and/or outdoor space is required. Appropriate dressing and shower facilities are needed.

Equipment and supplies: T-shirts, practice jerseys, athletic training/sports medicine supplies, appropriate sport paraphernalia, concession and merchandise items must all be on hand to use in the camp itself or to be given away and/or sold. Cash boxes are required for the concessions and souvenir booths. Posters, paper and paints are needed for promotional signs and flyers. A computer-generated list of all campers should be maintained to aid in tracking the progress of each camper and subsequent year's promotional and marketing efforts.

Publicity and promotion: A tasteful, computer-generated flyer, which serves as a reservation form, is created and distributed to area schools, athletic teams and coaches within easy driving distance. Posters should be displayed in area businesses. And pro bono promotional mention should be provided by the area news media, including the penny-savers. Secure business sponsors to donate money for souvenirs, which will have logos of both the business sponsor and the sponsoring organization.

Time: Planning and confirming the availability of the facilities, implementing extensive advertising activities and lining up the staffing necessary for the camp can take one to two months. Each camp lasts one week, Monday through Friday, 8 a.m. to 5 p.m. Allow 3-4 hours for general cleanup and final recordkeeping at the conclusion of each camp.

Expenditures: Allocate $500 seed money for this camp. While a so-called BIG NAME coach is a nice touch for a day camp, it is not absolutely necessary. Generally, area coaches can be secured for between $100-$150 per week plus free lodging and food from the concessions. The total cost of the staff, the rental of the facility, and advertising should be in the neighborhood of 35%-40% the gross income. Thus, with 100 youngsters attending the camp, there will be approximately $9,000 to $10,000 gross profit and a net profit of around $6,500. If a high school facility is used gratis or at minimal cost, the net profit picture is naturally greatly enhanced.

Personnel (Staff/Volunteers): The camp staff (12-18) consists of area high school and college coaches as well as volunteers (2-3) and staff (1-2) from the sponsoring organization. If eligibility rules permit, additional assistance can be provided by area college athletes. The staff to camper ratio should remain between 1-8 and 1-12. An athletic trainer or someone trained in first aid and should also be on hand throughout the week in addition to a few general supervisors.

RISK MANAGEMENT: There must be a plan of action in case campers are injured. The possibility of heat exhaustion or heat stroke, especially when the campers are playing outdoors, is very real and should be anticipated. The financial risks are minimal since the camp does not take place without a minimum of enrollees. The commitment to the camp staff and the rental of the site (if any) is contingent upon receipt of sufficient registrants.

PERMITS/LICENSES: It is necessary to check conference and state athletic rules and regulations which govern athletic camps and the eligibility of individual athletes. Similarly, there may be city, county and state regulations which cover day camps as well. In some locales the Department of Health might have responsibility for overseeing youth camps and clinics while in other communities the responsibility falls upon other offices such as the recreation department, etc.

HINTS: All campers receive a complimentary camp sport shirt. In baseball, soccer, basketball and volleyball camps each participant receives a miniature ball with the logos of the camp and sponsoring business on it. Such souvenirs become great advertisement tools when they are used by the camper long after the camp is over. Coaches forming the nucleus of the camp staff usually are successful in bringing or encouraging many of the students from their own school to attend. Care must be taken not to have such coaches actually teach/coach their own athletes when it is forbidden by various conference, state or national rules and regulations. At the end of the camp activities each camper receives a typed, individual assessment or evaluation form which outlines what the young athlete needs to work on in the future. In subsequent years, mass promotional mailings can be made directly to campers from prior years.

Fund raiser #47
Free Professional Car Wash

POTENTIAL NET INCOME: $6,000

COMPLEXITY/DEGREE OF DIFFICULTY: Low

DESCRIPTION: The owner of a professional drive-through car wash facility provides free washes for all vehicles on a Saturday while accepting donations on behalf of a recreation or sport organization. Some facilities can wash over 1000 cars on a single day. Donations averaging only $6 can generate over $6,000 in profit. In many instances, the profit can be significantly higher.

SCHEDULING: The all-day event should be scheduled on a spring, summer or fall day when plenty of sunshine is predicted.

RESOURCES:

Facilities: A professional car wash facility.

Equipment and supplies: All car wash items are contributed free by the owner of the facility. Signs need to be created promoting the special one-day event. Free donuts, coffee and soda should be provided for the drivers of the vehicles right next to a prominently displayed table containing a sign soliciting donations as well as a fish bowl (stuffed with $10 and $5 bills) where donations can be deposited.

Publicity and supplies: The success of this event really depends upon the advance publicity disseminated throughout the community. Signs placed strategically in various merchants' shop windows a week in advance coupled with placement of notices (gratis) in the area "penny-saver" (community newspaper) will help remind people. The publicity should center around the concept that the car wash is free and that donations, if any, will be going to a truly worthwhile purpose. If possible, specify how the contributions will be utilized. On the day of the car wash, volunteers can be stationed around town and in front of the car wash facility displaying large, professionally created signs publicizing the free car wash.

Time: The car wash is a one-day event only although the advance publicity takes place over a 2-3 week period. Planning for this event can be completed within a week or two.

Expenditures: The costs of the advertising and printing of the posters will be minimal, less than $50. Usually these can be secured without cost. The free refreshments to be given away will cost less than $100 if they cannot be donated. There are no other expenditures.

Personnel (Staff/Volunteers): The car wash facility can be staffed by 10-15 of the regularly paid personnel (paid by the owner) and/or volunteers and staff associated with the sport group. Another 15 volunteers and staff can be stationed near the facility as well as at other strategic locations within the community with signs advertising the event.

RISK MANAGEMENT: Insurance coverage is not a problem since the facility has coverage under the its blanket policy. One potential area of concern is the actual solicitation of donations. Great care should be taken lest car owners feel unduly pressured to donate. There is a difference between "hard sell" and being given the opportunity to contribute. The donations are not obligatory. There is no downside financial risk due to the nature of this fund raiser. The greatest risk is inclement weather in which case the event is rescheduled for a previously selected rain date.

PERMITS/LICENSES: None.

HINTS: Use "heavy hitters" (important and influential people) to approach the owner or manager of the car wash facility. In an attempt to obtain permission to use the facility emphasize the advantages accruing to the owner and the business in terms of (1) the excellent positive publicity for the car wash business due to the generosity of the owner, (2) increased exposure to the facility by first-time users of the car wash, and (3) the positive consequences accruing to the sport or recreation organization resulting from the financial contributions. After the event, a personal thank you letter to the owner is a fine touch. Also, prepare a typed release for the area news media explaining the event, the amount of money generated for the worthy cause, and an expression of appreciation to the owner of the facility. Always say "thanks" as publicly as possible.

Fund raiser #48
Lawn Mower Obstacle Race

POTENTIAL NET INCOME: $6,000

COMPLEXITY/DEGREE OF DIFFICULTY: Moderate

DESCRIPTION: An obstacle relay race using lawn mowers is organized by a sport or recreation organization. Prizes are given to the winning teams. The race consists of 16 laps, 4 each by a member of the 4-person relay teams. Organizers try to get local celebrities to be members of the racing crews or to be involved in some other capacity. Companies, organizations and individuals pay an entrance fee of $1,500 each to sponsor a team. A minimum of 4 and a maximum of 16 teams are allowed to race. If more than four teams are entered, teams are divided into groups of 3 or 4 with each race timed using a stop watch or portable scoreboard clock. Admission (both advance and day-of-race tickets) is $3 for adults and $1 for children. Additional profit is generated from the sale of concessions.

SCHEDULING: Since this is an outdoor event the race is scheduled when good weather is expected. The race is usually set for a Saturday or Sunday afternoon.

RESOURCES:

Facilities: A dirt or asphalt racetrack can be created on a parking lot or a deserted field. The course of the race can either be over a straightaway or involve curves. There should be adequate standing room for up to 2,000 spectators. Parking for these spectators also needs to be available.

Equipment and supplies: To time the event stop watches (and backups) or portable scoreboard clock is necessary. Riding lawn mowers and safety equipment for the drivers are provided by individual racing teams. An outdoor PA system is a must to help announce the progress of the race to the spectators. Prizes for winners are secured on a donated basis. All concession equipment and supplies are necessary plus chairs, tables and a portable tent to cover the concession area in the event of inclement weather. Signs, posters and flyers must be created to help spread the word about the race. Portable safety cones (to mark the course), tickets and cash boxes are needed.

Publicity and supplies: Teams and spectators for the big race are solicited through individual person-to-person contacts as well as by announcements through the area news media. Signs and posters are also distributed throughout the community and displayed in area businesses. Additionally, announcements over the sponsoring group's PA systems at other events help promote this important event.

Time: The event can be planned and organized within 2 weeks. It may take an additional 3-4 additional weeks to advertise for and solicit racing teams. Allow a total of 5 weeks for promotional and advertising efforts to attract the general public. Plan on spending 1-2 hours to set up the racecourse. The lawn mower race can take as long as 4 hours. Clean-up will take another 2 hours.

Expenditures: Allocate $500 in seed money. The concession stand will require $200 for beginning inventory. Plan on having another $100 in change each for the concession stand and the ticket booth. The site of the race as well as the concession stand's equipment and supplies should be available on a loan or donated basis. Budget $200 for promotional and advertising efforts, signs, safety cones and other odds and ends (i.e., prizes, if they are not donated).

Personnel (Staff/Volunteers): Volunteers (20-25) and staff (2-3) are required to sell both advance and day-of-race tickets. Some of these helpers are needed to personally approach and sign up potential racing teams (businesses, organizations and individuals). The concession stand should be staffed by rotating teams of 10 volunteers, on 2-hour shifts. A skilled master of ceremony to announce each race is a must.

RISK MANAGEMENT: Each rider is required to wear a safety helmet and overall. Additionally, blades must be removed from all lawn mowers prior to the race. Each racer is required to sign a hold harmless release statement. Make sure that the blanket insurance policy provides adequate coverage for this type of fund raising event. The financial risk is minimal as no significant expenditures are made until the racing teams are signed up and their entrance fees are collected.

PERMITS/LICENSES: Some communities require a special permit for concession stands. Check with the town clerk. Also, check with the town municipal offices to see whether a permit is needed to hold the lawn mower race itself, in light of the potential noise factor.

HINTS: Convincing local celebrities to take part in the race as drivers, sponsors or volunteers can play a big part in making this fund raiser a huge success. The publicity and promotional activities should center around the fact that this event is a fund raiser sponsored by a non-profit organization with the profits going to a worthy cause. Once the lawn mower race is a success, the race can easily become an annual affair.

Fund raiser #49
Sleigh Rides

POTENTIAL NET INCOME: $6,000

COMPLEXITY/DEGREE OF DIFFICULTY: Moderate

DESCRIPTION: During the winter months sleigh rides are provided over beautiful terrain. Horses pull the sleighs (or flatbed trailers) and/or tractors. Concessions operations are be erected both at the start of the trail and made available halfway through the trip. Tickets are $5 for adults and $2 for children (or whatever the market will bear).

SCHEDULING: This fund raiser is operational during the months of December and January. The operating hours for the sleigh rides are from 6 p.m. until midnight, Monday through Friday, and from 1 p.m. to midnight on weekends.

RESOURCES:

Facilities A suitable geographical area is needed over which a trail may be created to enable a sleigh or flatbed trailer to safely move. The trail should be of such a nature that the trip is entertaining and enjoyable for the participants as the sleighs are pulled through the scenic wonderland. A gently sloping area coupled with large, beautiful trees and vegetation is an ideal location. It should be located within easy driving distance (15-20 minutes) of a major population center.

Equipment and supplies: Sleighs, tractors or horses, Santa Claus costumes, Christmas music and a suitable outdoor sound system, portable heaters (for volunteers who work the ticket booth and the concession stands), outdoor spot lights, Christmas decorations, a portable phone (for emergencies), concession items and inventory (coffee, hot chocolate, donuts, cider and cookies), signs, posters, first aid kit, cash box, receipt and record books, and blankets are all needed. If sleighs are not readily available, promoters could substitute large flatbed trailers on which hay is placed.

Publicity and supplies: The promotional window for this fund raiser centers around 3-4 weeks prior to the start of the sleigh rides and continues until the ride operation is closed. Publicity should emphasize the opportunity to have a wonderful experience during this joyous season. Promote the rides as a family affair with both individual and group (with discount prices) rides available. Also, special prearranged rides may be scheduled at designated times. The public should be aware that the rides are sponsored by a non-profit entity. Notify schools and other youth organizations of the sleigh rides. Announcements and advertisements within the area's news media, including the pennysavers, is essential. Similarly, signs and posters should be displayed within area businesses, some of which could also serve as ticket outlets for advance sales. Announcements for the sleigh rides could also be made at other events sponsored by various groups.

Time: Planning time can take 2-3 weeks to line up the appropriate site, secure the sleighs (or flatbed trailers), the horses and/or tractors and organize all of the volunteers. Each sleigh ride takes approximately 30 minutes to complete. Plan on spending around 30 minutes to prepare for each day's activities as well as to close up shop after the last ride.

Expenditures: Anticipate spending $300 for promotional and publicity efforts. The use of the land, sleighs as well as horses or tractor should be on a loan basis. Another $150 is needed for concessions.

Personnel (Staff/Volunteers): Twenty to 25 volunteers and staff (each dressed as Santa Claus and/or helpers) are needed to drive the horses or the tractors at different times. All volunteers should be scheduled on a rotating basis so that no single individual is required to work more then 3-4 hours at a time. Also, volunteers (10-15) are involved in promoting and publicizing the sleigh rides, operating the concession stand, and selling advance tickets as well as tickets on site.

RISK MANAGEMENT: Check with the owner of the land to insure that adequate insurance coverage is in force for this type of fund raising activity. Train volunteers and staff in the handling of the horses and tractors. Have a volunteer on duty certified in first aid in case of an injury or accident. A portable phone is also recommended for emergencies.

PERMITS/LICENSES: Check with the town clerk or other municipal office to determine whether any permit or license is required in your community. Be sure to follow all health department rules and regulations regarding the operation of the concession stands.

HINTS: Whenever dealing with animals, have an expert handler on hand. Be sure to provide adequate care (food and water) and protection (have the vet's phone number handy just in case) for the animals at all times. Special group and party trips may also be promoted and conducted, thereby increasing profitability. This fund raising project can be successfully implemented even where snow is rare or non-existent if promoted as the "Snowless Sleigh Ride" (sleigh or flatbed trailer). In this instance, although the rides are conducted over snowless ground, the ride can still be enjoyable if suitable terrain is selected and there are adequate decorations and music available. The sleigh ride fund raiser can easily become a highly profitable, annual income-producing project.

Fund raiser #50
Great Duck Race

POTENTIAL NET INCOME: $7,000

COMPLEXITY/DEGREE OF DIFFICULTY: High

DESCRIPTION: Two thousand or more toy plastic ducks, each numbered consecutively, are released in a river or stream amidst great fanfare and are allowed to float towards a designated finish line. The ducks, priced at $5 apiece or seven for $25, are "sold" to individuals, businesses and organizations. "Owners" of the winning ducks earn donated prizes (cash, goods and services) for their owners. Entertainment (games, stories and/or a magic show) is provided for children prior to the start of the race. Additional income is generated from a concession stand.

SCHEDULING: The Great Duck Race can be scheduled at any time of the year when excellent weather is expected.

RESOURCES:

Facilities: A stream or river running at least a quarter mile is required. Ideally, the current should be sufficiently powerful to move the large number of plastic ducks downstream at a reasonable pace. The length of the waterway should be long enough so that the plastic ducks will have an opportunity to be spaced out from one another, enabling a clear winner to be declared.

Equipment and supplies: At least 2,000 toy ducks must be secured. Other items include permanent black paint and brushes (to number each toy duck), first aid kit, a canoe and paddles (to aid in retrieving ducks from the water), posters, flyers, signs, a portable PA system, rope (finish line), banners, tables, chairs, whistle, tickets and record/receipt books.

Publicity and supplies: Local newspapers should carry stories about the upcoming Great Duck Race and how to participate. Radio and television stations can include mention of this worthy fund raising project conducted by a local, non-profit organization. Businesses and organizations can display signs and posters publicizing and promoting the duck race. Utilize the PA systems and display posters at other sporting contests or recreation events conducted by the sponsoring organization. Vehicles parked at area malls and shopping centers can have attractive flyers placed on their windshields.

Time: This project can be planned and organized within a week. Securing permission to use the stream or river can take much longer. Waiting for the toy ducks to arrive from a wholesaler (at a steep discount, if not gratis) can take 3-4 weeks. Plan on spending several hours to set up the site at the starting line and another 2-3 hours for cleanup activities, including locating and retrieving all of the plastic ducks from the water and along the banks of the stream. The race can last for an hour or more.

Expenditures: $300 in seed money for promotional and publicity efforts and $200 for concession inventory is needed. If the plastic ducks are not donated, then allocate approximately 25 cents for each duck. Cash awards, if any, are paid from ticket sales.

Personnel (Staff/Volunteers): A large number of volunteers (50-60) and staff (2-4) are needed to make this fund raiser a success. Helpers are needed to organize and plan the event, secure necessary permissions and permits, paint numbers on the ducks, sell event tickets (ducks), staff the concession stand, maintain records, secure donated prizes, serve as race officials, PA announcers and as entertainers.

RISK MANAGEMENT: It is imperative that all of the plastic toy ducks be retrieved from the river or stream following the race. Prepare a well-conceived plan to locate and retrieve all of the ducks as part of your clean- up activities. Financial risks are significantly reduced by advance sales.

PERMITS/LICENSES: Permission may be required to utilize a river or stream for the Great Duck Race. In most communities there would be environmental concerns regarding the release of thousands of small plastic items into a free-flowing waterway. Contact the area conservation office or the local parks and recreation department. Secure permission from the malls' managers before placing flyers on the windshields of vehicles parked in their lots. A food permit may be required for the concession stand. Ask the town clerk, the community health department or other municipal offices for the requirements in your community.

HINTS: Since it takes almost as much work and money to run a race with only 500 ducks as it does with double or triple that number, organizers should attempt to sell as many as possible, both on an advance sale basis as well as on the day of the race itself. Instead of using toy ducks, table tennis balls may be utilized. However, there is something special about using toy ducks. Canoes or rowboats should be available to retrieve any plastic ducks hung up along the river banks after the race. Before the race, the portable PA system should be utilized to get the crown in a festive mood and, once the race is started, to keep onlookers appraised as to the status of the toy ducks. This fund raising project can easily become an annual affair. Organizers should attempt to store the plastic ducks for the following year's race.

Fund raiser #51
Rock-a-Thon

POTENTIAL NET INCOME: $7,450

COMPLEXITY/DEGREE OF DIFFICULTY: Low

DESCRIPTION: A large number of volunteers solicit pledges (from 10 cents to $1 an hour) based on how many hours the volunteers will sit in rocking chairs during a 36-hour period. Each donor is given a copy of the pledge sheet which clearly explains the rock-a-thon fund raiser and includes how much the donor has committed for each hour that the solicitor rocks. The volunteer rockers are given a 5-minute break each hour and may eat and drink whenever they wish, as long as they continue to rock. If 50 volunteers solicit an average of 15 donors, and if each donor's pledge averages merely $10, the net profit is $7,450 assuming that each solicitor lasts all 36 hours.

SCHEDULING: The rock-a-thon fund raiser may be scheduled at any time. It usually is scheduled to start early Friday evening and conclude at sometime mid-Sunday.

RESOURCES:

Facilities: Any large room such as a gymnasium or cafeteria will suffice. A conspicuous area within a popular shopping mall could also serve as the site.

Equipment and supplies: Rocking chairs, posters, flyers, signs, pledge sheets, record and receipt books as well as a boom box and a sound system. A television set, videotapes and books are made available to help entertain the rockers. Donated prizes are given away to those able to solicit the greatest contributions.

Publicity and supplies: Local newspapers and penny-savers should include publicity about the upcoming rock-a-thon. Area radio and television stations can also provide free public service announcements. Businesses and organizations within the community can display signs or posters. Organizers should use the PA system at other sport or recreation events to publicize the on-going solicitation of pledges. Sign-up of pledges can even be done at these events. Highlight that this is a fund raising effort sponsored by a local, non-profit organization. Also, reveal how the net profits will be spent. Photos should be taken of the volunteers during the rock-a-thon for possible inclusion within various newspaper articles following the event. These photos can also be used in subsequent years' rock-a-thons.

Time: This fund raising project can be planned and organized within a week or two. Reserve the site where the actual rocking chairs can be set up well in advance. Advance publicity should be completed within a 3-5 week period during which the solicitation of pledges should also take place. The rock-a-thon itself should last for a 36-hour period over a weekend. Volunteers should collect all donations over a single weekend after the event.

Expenditures: The rock-a-thon can be initiated with $50 seed money. All of the rocking chairs and most of the other supplies can be obtained on a loan or free basis.

Personnel (Staff/Volunteers): A large number of volunteers (50-75) and staff (1-2) is needed to make this fund raiser a success. The key to the success of this event is the successful solicitation of many pledges.

RISK MANAGEMENT: There is little downside financial risk since there are few expenses involved. Organizers should anticipate that approximately 80% to 85% of the pledges will actually be converted into cash. In all fund raising efforts involving pledges it is rare if more than 90% of the pledges are actually converted to cash contributions. The liability exposure is kept to a minimum as long as donors are clearly aware of how much they have committed themselves. Also, check that the insurance policy covering the site is adequate.

PERMITS/LICENSES: Permission must be secured from the owners of the site prior to seeking the pledges.

HINTS: Be sure that individuals who make pledges understand their maximum financial exposure. No one wants to have an embarrassing situation in which a potential donor is surprised or shocked to learn how much one's pledge actually commits them to donate. To help keep the rockers entertained and fight boredom during the lengthy marathon, some organizers make available background music, good books and magazines as well as a videotape or two.

Fund raiser #52
Can and Bottle Collection

POTENTIAL NET INCOME: $7,500 annually

COMPLEXITY/DEGREE OF DIFFICULTY: Moderate

DESCRIPTION: Youngsters and other volunteers collect empty soda and beer bottles and cans to be returned to merchants, and the refundable deposit retrieved goes to the charitable cause. One such company is Town Pump Recyclers, 871 Attridge, Churchville, New York (716-293-1725). The collection can take two forms: either door-to-door collection efforts or choosing one or more central collection sites where the public can drop off cans and bottles. Then the organizers can sort and bag the bottles and cans and take them to the recycler in exchange for the deposits.

SCHEDULING: This fund raiser can be initiated at any time of the year. In point of fact, the collection can be scheduled three times during the calendar year to provide maximum profit for the sport or recreation organization. Door-to-door solicitation is facilitated if the collection is held during nice weather.

RESOURCES:

Facilities One or more central collection sites is needed where the public can drop off cans and bottles. An indoor storage area is also needed to keep the cans and bottles until there is a sufficient number to be taken to the recycling center.

Equipment and supplies: Bags to carry and store the bottles and cans are required. Also, posters and signs should be created. Vehicles are needed to transport the bottles and cans to the recycling center.

Publicity and supplies: Announcements in the area news media, both print and electronic, can be most helpful in getting the word out to the general public. Utilize the PA system at other events sponsored by the organizing group as well as at the events of other organizations and groups. Signs and posters can be displayed in area businesses. Highlight the non-profit nature of this fund raising effort and how the profit will be put to good use within the community. Of course, there should be a highly visible sign at the central collection site.

Time: This fund raiser can be planned and organized within a week. The actual collection process (door-to-door and the establishment of a central receiving area) can be spread over 3-4 weeks, three times a year.

Expenditures: This fund raiser can be initiated with less than $50 for bags, signs and posters.

Personnel (Staff/Volunteers): The more volunteers involved in the collection process the better. A fund raising group consisting of 50- 75 volunteers (both youngsters and adults) can reap big dividends if they effectively canvas a large area of a community. Some of these same volunteers can be assigned responsibility of overseeing the central collection site(s) and the storage of the bottles and cans until they are taken to recycling center. Adult volunteers are needed to oversee the sorting, counting and packaging of the cans and bottles as well as their packaging for transportation to the recycling center.

RISK MANAGEMENT: There is no financial risk involved. The legal liability exposure can be reduced if a training session is held for the youngsters who will be traveling door-to-door collecting the bottles and cans. The training session should emphasize both safety aspects of traveling from house to house as well as the proper (polite) method of asking for donations of the bottles and cans. In terms of safety factors, youngsters should collect bottles while traveling in pairs and should not venture into strange neighborhoods or solicit items after dark unless accompanied by an adult.

PERMITS/LICENSES: Some communities require door-to-door solicitors to secure a peddler's permit or a hawker's license. Check with the town clerk or bureau of licenses. Doublecheck with the recycling center to insure that the bottles and cans are properly sorted and bagged to be accepted.

HINTS: This fund raiser is only applicable where refundable deposits are required to be paid on soda and/or beer bottles or cans. In New York, for example, there is a 5-cent deposit paid on every bottle or can purchased. Over a period of four months it is not unreasonable to expect to retrieve over 50,000 bottles and cans for a profit of $2,500, depending upon the number of volunteers involved. Conducting this fund raising event three times each year can net the organizers over $7,500. Adults should be handle all money received and make a periodic financial report to the organization.

Fund raiser #53
Race to a Healthy Lifestyle

POTENTIAL NET INCOME: $7,500

COMPLEXITY/DEGREE OF DIFFICULTY: High

DESCRIPTION: 200-300 racers participate in a cross-country run/walk over a predetermined course (2 to 4 kilometers), raising funds for a worthy cause sponsored by a well-known, local non-profit organization. The run/walk race is billed as *"The Race to a Healthy Lifestyle."* An entry fee of $25 is charged to each race participant, who in turn receives a colorful T-shirt in memory of the event. Participants may pay the entire entry fee themselves or may solicit pledges and contributions from others, individuals and/or organizations. Prizes may be awarded for any number of accomplishments. However, the emphasis of the race is not so much on competition as it is on participation and the generation of monies for a worthy cause.

SCHEDULING: The event can be held on any Saturday or Sunday afternoon when excellent weather is anticipated. A rain date, in the event of inclement weather, is publicized in advance.

RESOURCES:

Facilities: The course can be in a rural, suburban or city setting, or any combination. The start of the race should be at an area where the large group of participants can congregate together at one time. Adequate parking is a must. First aid stations can be situated at strategic places along the racecourse as well as at the finish line.

Equipment and supplies: T-shirts, tables, chairs, a cash box, pencils, entry forms, a record book, paper race numbers, safety pins, prizes, signs, posters, first aid kits and portable water coolers and paper cups.

Publicity and supplies: Advance publicity is a must if this fund raising project is to be successful. The emphasis should be on how individuals can achieve a healthy lifestyle while also helping a worthy cause. The immediate challenge is to make people in the community aware of the race and then to interest 200-300 to run or walk. In addition, promotional and publicity efforts should be successful in convincing others to sponsor one or more individuals. Thus it is important that area newspapers and penny-savers carry announcements explaining not only about the race itself but how the non-profit organizing group will put the money to good use. Public service announcements might even be aired by radio and television stations. Local businesses and organizations can display signs and posters promoting the event. Some can even serve as advance ticket outlets for the race.

Time: The race can be planned and organized within 7-10 days. Attracting a sufficiently large number of participants can take as long as 5-6 weeks. During this time solicitation of donated prizes and other equipment and supplies can be completed. Preparation on race day, including accepting race registrations, can take 3-4 hours. The race itself can take 3 hours. Allocate an hour to clean up afterwards.

Expenditures: Most of the items needed can be loaned or donated. Even the T-shirts can be solicited as a donation from a local wholesaler or manufacturer. If purchased, the T-shirts should be bought at a deep discount, $2 to $3 apiece. The event can be kicked off with $250 in seed money, most of which is spent publicizing and promoting the event.

Personnel (Staff/Volunteers): Medical personnel (a NATA trainer, a nurse, or a trained EMT) should be available on the day of the race. Additional volunteers (10-15) and staff (2-4) are needed to plan, organize and implement the day's activities.

RISK MANAGEMENT: The availability of appropriately stationed rest stops (with water, chairs, first aid kits and medical staff) will help minimize potential serious injuries among the racers and walkers. Financial risks are minimal if advance entry fees are collected by the organizers. Prior to the start of the race, organizers should pass out information sheets outlining the race course. These sheets should also have pertinent information regarding the health and safety aspects of participating.

PERMITS/LICENSES: Be sure to secure permission to run the racecourse through (or over) private or public lands. Police authorities may have to be notified if the race course will transverse public streets.

HINTS: Be sure to thank all involved in the fund raiser, including those who walked/ran the course, those who pledged and donated money, those who planned and organized the event, and those who helped administer the event. Some organizers plan for a large social gathering–such as a tail-gate party–at the conclusion of the event. If you do this, it is necessary to have the finish line at a site conducive to such an event, such as a large parking lot or a park. Food and drink and other paraphernalia should be donated by area businesses.

Fund raiser #54
Social Pyramid

POTENTIAL NET INCOME: $7,700

COMPLEXITY/DEGREE OF DIFFICULTY: Low

DESCRIPTION: A series of social gatherings planned so that supporters and the public can contribute to the financial wellbeing of the organization while having an enjoyable time in an informal setting. This fund raising effort starts with five of the organization's officers and/or staff members hosting individual parties in their own homes, such as a sit-down dinner, a brunch, a card party or watching Monday night football on television with pizzas, pretzels and pop. Each party is paid for by the host(s) and the guests contribute $10, that goes directly into the organization's fund raising kitty. The social pyramid continues with each of these original guests in turn hosting some type of gathering for five other supporters and friends of the organization. And, in turn, these guests will donate $10 each and agree to host (and pay for) their own party, and for five other individuals, each of whom is expected to donate $10 to the organization. Thus, with only four levels of the social pyramid there will be a total of 155 food gatherings or parties involving 775 different individuals. This translates to a gross profit of $7,750 if each individual contributes a minimum of $10. Of course, the guests who attend the last level of parties only need contribute $10 as they will not be expected to host parties themselves. Thus, the last group of guests typically involve less ardent supporters of the organization who might feel comfortable only donating $10.

SCHEDULING: The different gatherings can take place anytime, and should be scheduled during a 2-4 month time period so as not to drag out the fund raising but yet allow time for the various parties to be adequately planned and implemented.

RESOURCES:

Facilities: Individual homes will serve as the party sites.

Equipment and supplies: All necessary equipment and supplies will be provided (donated) by the host(s) of each individual gathering.

Publicity and supplies: Publicity can be achieved through announcements in area newspapers and pennysavers. Announcements in the printed programs and/or newsletters of the sponsoring organization can be very effective. Don't forget to utilize the PA system at different events to make suitable and timely announcements. Be sure to publicize how the profits will be spent.

Time: This fund raising project can be planned and organized within 2-3 weeks. But 2-4 months can be involved before the last of the parties are concluded. Each gathering can last from 2-3 hours.

Expenditures: This project can be initiated with less than $50.

Personnel (Staff/Volunteers): Success of this fund raising effort is dependent upon volunteers and staff willing to host a party for at least five other individuals. Initially, this involves five dedicated individuals whose parties will involve a total of 25 other individuals. These 25 will in turn host gatherings involving a total of 125 people, and so on. By the end, 775 individuals will be involved in this on-going fund raising effort. Of this number, 155 volunteers need to be willing to plan and host their own party or gathering. Appoint a chairperson(s) to keep track of the various parties and to assist with or coordinate the invitation process so that no one individual is invited to more than one party, and yet all appropriate individuals actually receive one invitation to a gathering.

RISK MANAGEMENT: There is no financial risk since all costs are donated by those individuals hosting their individual parties for their five guests. Legal exposure is also negligible for the organization. However, those individuals hosting parties are legally responsible for what transpires at their individual gatherings. Hence, great care must be taken lest the serving of alcoholic beverages results in a tragic accident. Some groups prohibit alcohol at these gatherings while others leave the decision up to the individual hosts.

PERMITS/LICENSES: None.

HINTS: It is important that the invitations be crystal clear: acceptance of a party invitation means a $10 donation to the sponsoring organization. And for 155 individuals (the first 3 levels of the social pyramid), it is necessary to also host their own party for five other individuals. One of the objectives is to increase the sphere of influence and association of the organization within the community. These series of food gatherings are an excellent way to meet new friends and to garner greater support (moral and financial) for the non-profit organization.

Fund raiser #55
"There's A Man in the Kitchen" Cookbook

POTENTIAL NET INCOME: $7,800

COMPLEXITY/DEGREE OF DIFFICULTY: Moderate

DESCRIPTION: A cookbook with a variety of delicious recipes submitted entirely by men is published by a charitable organization. It could be called, *"There's A Man in the Kitchen."* Each contributor is asked to provide name; phone number; best time to be reached; address; position, title and organization; title and category of the recipe(s); comments, such as suggestions for complementing dishes, preparation time. The recipes can be for appetizers, sandwiches, soups, salads, seafood, meats, poultry, vegetables, casseroles, breads and rolls, low-calorie and low-fat dishes, desserts (pies, pastries, cakes, candies and cookies) and beverages. With 125-150 recipes, the soft-cover publication can sell for $10.

SCHEDULING: The cookbook may be sold at any time of the year.

RESOURCES:

Facilities: A site is needed for the publication's creation. This can be an office, a bedroom or even a basement. Also, a storage site is needed for unsold books to be safely stored.

Equipment and supplies: Organizers should secure use of a computer with desktop publishing software. The entire cookbook with illustrations can be created on a personal computer, ready to be submitted to the publisher. Both order forms and submission forms must also be created or purchased.

Publicity and supplies: Individual solicitations of culinary specialties can be made on a person-to-person basis. Additionally, publicity inviting submissions of recipes can be included in local newspapers and penny-savers. Even the public address systems at sporting contests and recreation events can be used to request additional recipes for the cookbook. To sell the cookbooks, utilize newspapers and pennysavers. Local radio and television stations might provide free publicity as part of their Public Service Announcements (PSAs). Area businesses and organizations can also display signs and posters promoting the cookbook. Some can even sell the publication. Be sure to highlight the fact that this is a fund raising project sponsored by a worthy, local non-profit organization. Reveal how the profits will be put to use within the community.

Time: Allow 2 to 3 months for the collection of recipes. Collating and organizing the recipes and putting the book together, including the printing process, can take another 3-4 weeks. The selling window for the cookbook should be 3 to 4 weeks prior to the actual publication (advance sales) and 5-6 weeks of concerted selling efforts following publication. Of course, unsold copies may be marketed throughout the year until the inventory is depleted.

Expenditures: For books selling for $10, plan on spending approximately $2 to have each book published. Allocate $200 seed money for initial publicity and promotional expenses. Thus, if 1,000 books are published the net profit is about $7,800. Of course, the greater the number of books published, the lower the publication cost per cookbook.

Personnel (Staff/Volunteers): Volunteers (25-30) and staff (2-5) will solicit recipes as well as help in marketing and selling the books. Computer literate helpers (2-3) can be of great help in putting the publication together. Volunteers (3-5) are also needed to serve as proofreaders and editors to insure that the final version is indeed first-rate.

RISK MANAGEMENT: Advance sales reduce the downside financial risks. Men who donate recipes should be willing (if approached properly) to purchase a copy for themselves or for a gift for someone else. Thus, if the cookbook contains recipes from 130 individuals, it is safe to assume that at least 100 cookbooks will be purchased (on an advance basis) by those who contributed recipes. This generates $1,000 in money up-front to help defray the publishing expenses. Legal liability is minimal as long as the recipes submitted are original and not copied from other publications.

PERMITS/LICENSES: If the cookbook is sold door-to-door, you may need a peddlers permit or hawkers license. Check with the town clerk or the local or municipal bureau of licensing.

HINTS: Securing a company that can publish the cookbook at a reasonable price and within an acceptable time frame can be accomplished in several ways. First, check with print shops at nearby colleges or universities. They may be willing to take on the project at a reasonable cost when their presses are not being heavily utilized. Second, contact so-called vanity presses (look in the phone book under publishers). These are companies that specialize in publishing, for a fee, personalized books for individuals and organizations. Third, contact a regular printing company, or even a local quick/fast print shop to compare costs.

Fund raiser #56
Day of Game Drawing

POTENTIAL NET INCOME: $8,000

COMPLEXITY/DEGREE OF DIFFICULTY: Low.

DESCRIPTION: A raffle is held at the end of each athletic contest or recreation activity. Each raffle ticket costs only $1, with 6 tickets for $5. A variety of items and services may be raffled. Local businesses and corporations are approached for donations.

SCHEDULING: This fund raising effort can be initiated at any time. One significant item (value in the neighborhood of $75+ retail) is raffled off at the end of each sporting event/recreational activity.

RESOURCES:

Facilities: No special facilities are required.

Equipment and supplies: Use of a microphone and sound system is required. Also a large fish bowl or other suitable container is necessary to hold ticket stubs and from which to draw the winning ticket. A table to display the item being raffled off should be available for all to see.

Publicity and supplies: There are two aspects of publicity and promotion. First, promote the drawing to potential donors of major gifts to be raffled off. Second, entice individuals to buy the raffle tickets. Highlight the non-profit nature of the sponsor and the worthiness of the activities, and how the money will be spent. The periodic drawing should be publicized and promoted continuously during the time when the drawings are taking place. Local businesses should display signs highlighting the next raffle's BIG PRIZE. Similarly, the drawing should be promoted at all other events of the sponsoring entity. On the night of the drawings, display the prizes prominently. If the prize is a service, such as a year's free car wash at a local establishment or a get-away weekend at Holiday Inn, then a sign and/or picture of the prize should be displayed.

Time: Planning can be completed within a week. Getting the donated prizes will take considerably longer. Plan on at least 4-5 weeks of concentrated effort.

Expenditures: This fund raiser can be kicked off with less than $50 for signs and posters.

Personnel (Staff/Volunteers): Volunteers (10-12) to solicit the prizes on an individual, person-to-person, basis from individuals and businesses. These volunteers should be substantial members of the community who will have little difficulty gaining access to other important decision makers.

RISK MANAGEMENT: There are few downside risks involving either finances or legal liability exposure. The only real risk is that insufficient meaningful prizes will be obtained to be raffled at each of the events. Thus, it is imperative that all, or almost all, of the gifts and prizes to be raffled off be obtained or pledged prior to the initial announcement of periodic raffle drawings.

PERMITS/LICENSES: Since this fund raiser is a form of gambling, some communities require the sponsoring organization to secure a gambling or game of chance license. Check with the town clerk or municipal offices.

HINTS: This is a very easy fund raiser to conduct as long as a sufficient number of meaningful prizes can be solicited. If the sponsoring organization has 30-35 different contests or events throughout the year and the average net profit from each raffle is $250, the annual take can range between $7,500-$8,700.

Fund raiser #57
Souvenir Sport Paraphernalia Auction

POTENTIAL NET INCOME: $10,000

COMPLEXITY/DEGREE OF DIFFICULTY: Moderate

DESCRIPTION: Letters are sent to college and university athletic teams as well as professional sports teams requesting a donation on behalf of one's non- profit organization. The donation could be an item or two of equipment or a souvenir with that team's logo or name for an auction. The letter should be on official letterhead and include the signatures of several of the most in-influential people associated with the fund raising project. The letter should detail the purpose of the fund raising effort and the worthiness of the project. If available, some type of professional literature or publication that would lend credence to the fund raising organization and the request for souvenirs should be included.

SCHEDULING: The solicitation of the used and/or new souvenirs (helmets, caps, shoes, shirts, shorts, autograph pictures, key chains, socks, etc.) can be an ongoing effort during the year. The event itself can be scheduled as a stand-alone event or may be piggy-backed upon another activity such as a dinner dance, a recreational meeting or sport banquet.

RESOURCES:

Facilities: Facility needs are dependent upon the type of event being planned in conjunction with the raffle. If a dinner or luncheon is planned, then a suitable dining facility with adequate parking is required. Hopefully, the combined event will attract 250-300. Of course, there is a need for space to store the souvenir items collected until the event.

Equipment and supplies: Display tables and racks to show off the items is a must as is an excellent sound system. Signs, flyers, poster displays and "thank-you" notes are needed.

Publicity and supplies: The availability of highly desirable souvenirs forms the cornerstone of the publicity and promotional campaign. Announcements in area news media listing some of the souvenirs available combined with signs displayed in area businesses can pay big dividends. Don't forget about flyers placed on windshields of vehicles parked in area malls and shopping centers. Highlight how the money will be spent.

Time: Planning and solicitation of the souvenirs can consume up to 9 months and should be spread throughout the year. The disposition of the items can be concluded within 60 to 90 minutes.

Expenditures: There will be mailing and phone costs associated with this fund raiser but these will be minimal in light of the potential profits. Frequently, both mailing and phone expenses can be absorbed (donated) by sympathetic individuals or companies. Plan on spending less than $300 in seed money.

Personnel (Staff/Volunteers): Volunteers (5-10) are needed to solicit souvenirs and to plan for the auction or sale. If an auction is planned, then a professional auctioneer should be obtained either on a free or reduced cost basis. Also, individual contact via phone, letter or in person is highly recommended whenever a booster or fan of the fund raising organization has a personal contact with someone associated with a particular professional or a college team. Even if no personal contact exists, a personal phone call from an important personage associated with the fund raising organization, following the mailing of the solicitation letter, will often pay big dividends. The number of additional volunteers (20-25) needed depends upon what type of special event is planned to coincide with the auction.

RISK MANAGEMENT: There is little downside risk in the solicitation of souvenirs. The worst that can happen is that a college or professional team will not send or donate anything. Since the auction or sale of items would not be advertised or even mentioned publicly until a sufficient number of quality items are received, there is no embarrassment should the solicitation efforts meet with less than sterling success. Organizers must make those who bid on the souvenirs aware that the items must be treated only as souvenirs—they are not suitable for actual athletic competition. For example, a used football helmet donated by a team should never be used to actually play football because it is no longer certified as a safe helmet.

PERMITS/LICENSES: None.

HINTS: If this is to be an annual fund raising effort, letters seeking donations should only be sent to 25% or 33% of the total population of the university and professional teams. In this way it will be 2 or 3 years before the same teams are "hit" with another request from the same fund raising group. One would not want to wear out one's welcome by asking a team every year for souvenirs. If the college or professional team did previously contribute, this fact should be mentioned in subsequent letters. Similarly, whenever an organization does donate a souvenir item, send a personal thank-you note.

Fund raiser #58
Adult (Co-Ed) Fast-Pitch Softball Tournament

POTENTIAL NET INCOME: $10,000

COMPLEXITY/DEGREE OF DIFFICULTY: High

DESCRIPTION: A fast pitch, double elimination, adult softball tournament, involving 32 teams, is conducted by a recreation or sport organization. A general admission fee of $1 is charged for adult spectators for each game (with the exception of the championship match-up) while children under 12 are admitted free. For the title game, adults are charged $2.50 and youngsters over 6, $1. Each team is charged a $150 entry fee. The first place team wins $1,000 in cash, while the second team earns $500, and the third place team receives $250. A variety of donated prizes and trophies are awarded to individuals and teams based upon outstanding performances. Local businesses and organizations are sought as sponsors of the tournament and contributors of between $250-$500. If only 15 business agree to be sponsors and contribute an average of $300, the tournament coffers will be enriched by an additional $4,500. An additional $3,000 can easily be realized from concession operations.

SCHEDULING: The softball tournament can be scheduled any time during the late spring, summer or early fall. Individual games can be scheduled throughout the week or may be restricted to weekends only. Both day and night games may be scheduled if lights are available.

RESOURCES:

Facilities: A number of regulation softball fields should be made available (on a donated basis) so that more than one game at a time can be played. Adequate number of seats must be available to allow sizeable crowds to view the games. If lights are available then evening games are possible. Adequate and safe parking is a must.

Equipment and supplies: Signs, posters, flyers, tables, chairs, tickets, baseball lining equipment and paint, balls, bats, bases and as well as concession items such as paper plates, napkins, cups, condiments, food and drink are needed.

Publicity and supplies: Advance publicity can consist of invitations sent out to selected area fast pitch softball teams. Promotional signs can be placed in various recreation and sport facilities as well as in local businesses in an effort to attract competitors as well as spectators. Advance tickets can be sold at these locations. Area newspapers as well as local radio and television stations can play a large role in disseminating information about the tournament, before, during and after the competition. Announcements at other sporting and recreation events can also be most effective in getting the word out. Don't forget to highlight the fact that this is a fund raising project conducted by a worthy non-profit organization. Publicize how the profits will be spent.

Time: The tournament can be planned and organized within a week or two. Efforts to sign up the 32 teams can take as long as 3-5 weeks, if not longer. Other publicity and promotional efforts, including advance ticket sales, should be limited to 3-4 weeks.

Expenditures: Allocate $1,000 in seed money. Prize money totals $1,750 which can be paid from the profits. Organizers should not be bashful about soliciting skilled personnel to volunteer their services, such as officials, scorers, scoreboard operators, etc. Similarly, non-cash prizes and awards for the players and teams can be sought on a pro bono basis. Every dollar saved is truly a dollar earned.

Personnel (Staff/Volunteers): Volunteers (25-35) and staff (2-4) are needed to organize the tournament, solicit sponsors, secure donated prizes and awards, staff the concession stand and perform any number of other tasks normally associated with the conducting of a sports tournament. Additional helpers are needed to volunteer as umpires, scorers, timers, announcers and scoreboard operators.

RISK MANAGEMENT: Legal liability exposure can be kept to a minimum if normal safety rules are adhered to in terms of home event management of the softball contests. Check with the insurer of the fields to be used to ensure that the blanket insurance policy covering the site(s) will protect the sponsoring organization and its agents (volunteers and paid personnel).

PERMITS/LICENSES: Some communities require a food permit or license in order to operate a concession stand. Check with the local health department or town clerk to see what is necessary.

HINTS: Effective media coverage throughout the tournament can be very effective in increasing attendance at the games. It is very important that officials and umpires are qualified and competent. If qualified umpires are not available on a donated basis, organizers must pay to secure competent umps. Inferior officiating can put a damper on a tournament of this nature. At first it may be necessary to stage a 16-team tournament rather than a 32-team affair. Once this tournament gets off the ground, subsequent softball fund raisers will be even more successful.

Fund raising projects to generate over $10,000

5

Chapter 5

Fund raising projects to generate over $10,000

Fund raiser #59
Barbecue Extravaganza

POTENTIAL NET INCOME: $11,000

COMPLEXITY/DEGREE OF DIFFICULTY: High

DESCRIPTION: Tickets are sold for $50 each, with profits going to a recognized worthwhile cause. Plan for 400-500 tickets to be sold.

SCHEDULING: The barbecue is scheduled for the spring of each year.

RESOURCES:

Facilities: Almost any pleasant outdoor site will suffice. Sufficient parking is also required.

Equipment and supplies: Cooking paraphernalia such as gas or charcoal grills, utensils, etc., are necessary as are plastic cups, plates, forks, knives, spoons, paper napkins and tickets. In case of inclement weather, a large tent should be available or plans made to move inside a building. Tables, colorful decorations, paper tablecloths, and chairs are also needed as are large buckets with ice to keep the drinks cold. Signs, flyers and posters need to be created.

Publicity and promotion: Promotional activities revolve around the worthiness of the fund raising project itself, that is, how the money is to be used within the community. Announcements can be made by the local news media, including area pennysavers. Local businesses and organizations can display posters and signs. Some of these businesses can even serve as advance ticket outlets. Flyers can be placed on vehicles parked in area malls and shopping centers.

Time: The barbecue can be planned and organized within a 2-week period. However, allow 6-8 weeks for the details to be ironed out:

reserving the facility, promoting the event and then selling advance tickets. The selling window (tickets) should not exceed 4-5 weeks. Both set-up and clean-up activities will take 2-3 hours. The event lasts from 11 a.m. to 7 p.m.

Expenditures: Organizers should solicit all of the food and drink on a free or greatly reduced cost basis—due to the non-profit nature of the fund raising. Similarly, the cooking equipment, supplies, and items such as chairs, tables, etc., should be donated or loaned. The use of the physical site should also be free. Plan on spending $500 for promotional efforts, including limited advertisements within area newspapers and over the more popular radio stations. Other costs should be kept below $500.

Personnel (Staff/Volunteers): There are three essential elements—all involving people, both volunteers and staff—to the success of this fund raising project. One is the ability to secure the site, food, drink and other items on a free or greatly reduced basis. The second is the ability to sell a sufficient number of tickets and promote the barbecue to the public. And the last involves adequately staffing the extravaganza in terms of set-up tasks, food preparation and serving, taking tickets, etc., and clean-up activities. There should be 30-50 volunteers and 2-4 staff members actively involved.

RISK MANAGEMENT: The financial risk is greatly diminished if the food and drink items are donated. To keep legal liability to a minimum, be sure that all rules and regulations governing food storage, preparation and serving are strictly observed. Similarly, check the blanket insurance policy of the site to insure that adequate coverage is in existence.

PERMITS/LICENSES: Obtain permission to distribute flyers on cars and trucks parked in area malls and shopping centers. It may also be necessary to secure a food permit or license. Check with the local health department and/or town clerk.

HINTS: In some instances, it may be necessary to pay for food and drink and other items of equipment and supplies. Also, there might be a rental fee (hopefully insignificant) incurred. If any of these costs must be paid by the sponsors, there are two options available to the organizers. First, to increase the ticket price to the general public so that the $35 profit per ticket can be maintained. Second, to keep the ticket price the same and accept a lower net profit for each ticket sold. In essence, local conditions will determine just how much the tickets can be sold for. Price tickets in light of what the market will bear. After all, raising the ticket price significantly will have the adverse effect of eliminating some potential patrons from participating. It might be better to have more people involved even if it means a little less profit. Once this event has become a success, it can easily become "bigger and better" each year. Some organizers even plan this event twice a year, once in the fall and again in the spring.

Fund raiser #60
Rodeo Festival

POTENTIAL NET INCOME: $11,000

COMPLEXITY/DEGREE OF DIFFICULTY: High

DESCRIPTION: The sponsor contracts with a professional organizer of rodeos to put on a show(s). Profits from the rodeo are generated from gate receipts, sponsorships from local merchants (signs displayed in the facility and advertisements in the programs) and from the sale of concessions, programs, and appropriate merchandise associated with the sponsoring organization.

SCHEDULING: Weekend afternoons and/or evenings are highly popular. If the event is outdoors, the weather can be a real factor. The organizers should schedule when the weather is usually cooperative and attempt to sell as many advance tickets (at a discount) as possible. Naturally, tickets on the day of the rodeo are sold. But advance ticket sales will determine whether or not the event will be successful.

RESOURCES:

Facilities: An appropriate outdoor or indoor site is a must. There must be appropriate seating for large numbers. Adequate and safe parking is required. So too are clean restrooms or outdoor port-a-pots. If indoors, the facility must have a dirt surface. The rodeo professionals will be able to tell the sponsoring group exactly what is needed for the facility.

Equipment and supplies: Other than the items used in promoting and marketing the event and equipment and supplies used in selling concessions and sport merchandise, all necessary equipment and supplies are provided by the professional rodeo people.

Publicity and promotion: Extensive publicity and promotional efforts are a must, including numerous point-of-sale ticket outlets. Paid advertisements and gratis announcements in the print media as well as public service announcements (PSAs) by radio and/or television stations are essential. Advertising from area merchants can be sold for signs displayed in the facility as well as ads placed within the program (which are printed and then distributed on the day of the event). Group discount sales (schools, churches, businesses, Boy and Girl Scouts, other youth groups, etc.) should be a high priority. Promote the event as a family affair.

Time: Planning and coordinating the details can take 5-6 months. There might be 2 shows on the same day or more spread over two days, depending upon the anticipated demand by the public. Each show can run from 2-3 hours. It is suggested that the so-called selling window for advance tickets be no longer than 5-6 weeks. Taking longer to sell advance tickets is not overly productive since most of the tickets will be sold within the 3-4 weeks prior to the deadline anyway.

Expenditures: Plan on spending around $200 for posters and signs and paid advertisements as well as $150 in start-up funds for the concession stand(s). The costs of the programs to be sold will be covered by the ads from sponsors. The rental cost of the indoor or outdoor site can range from as little as $250 a day to as much as $1,000 a day or more. Remember, the professional rodeo group is in the business of making money. That group either takes a percentage of the gross ticket sales or accepts a flat fee, between $1,500 and $3,000, depending upon the travel time involved and the number of shows conducted. It is imperative that there be a date agreed upon by both professional rodeo organizers and the sponsoring group, by which the rodeo event can be cancelled if insufficient advance tickets have been sold.

Personnel (Staff/Volunteers): Most of the personnel connected with the operation are provided by the rodeo group. A sizeable number of the sport staff (2-3) and volunteers (50-55) are needed for selling tickets, running the concessions and merchandise booths and handling the details or mechanics of the operation such as parking, seating, site preparation and cleanup, etc.

RISK MANAGEMENT: Insurance coverage (liability) must be checked out for protecting the sponsoring sport entity as well as the owners of the property on which the rodeo will be held. The professional rodeo organization should post a bond of at least $1 million and provide references, which should be thoroughly checked before a contract is signed. To prevent accusations (and resultant negative publicity), some organizers recommend that local representatives of the Society for the Prevention of Cruelty to Animals (SPCA) be consulted when planning the event. They reason that this helps forestall potential criticism in terms of perceptions of mistreatment of the animals. The downside financial risks of this fund raising project can be severe.

PERMITS/LICENSES: None.

HINTS: Securing a reputable rodeo group is the first order of business followed by securing an adequate facility. The ultimate success of the fund raising project depends upon the amount of advance tickets that can be sold. It cannot be overemphasized that there is a need to select, in advance, a date by which the rodeo can be called off (without further financial obligations to any party) if there are insufficient ticket sales to warrant continuing the effort. For example, if the costs of the rodeo are approximately $3,500 and the ticket sales have generated only $3,000 by the arbitrary cut-off date, then it might be wise to cancel the project. One way to protect the sponsoring group is to have an individual booster or business owner agree, in writing, to cover any losses, up to a certain specified amount, incurred should there be insufficient ticket sales.

Fund raiser #61
Three-on-Three (Co-Ed) Basketball Tournament

POTENTIAL NET INCOME: $11,000

COMPLEXITY/DEGREE OF DIFFICULTY: High

DESCRIPTION: A co-educational, three on three, half-court, basketball tournament is presented at both indoor and outdoor locations throughout the community. Each team consists of four players. Tournament play is scheduled for male teams, female teams and co-educational teams. Competition is also broken down into several categories: (1) open division, (2) senior (over 50 years of age), (3) collegiate, (4) high school, and (5) no formal playing experience. Each game is played to 11 baskets, with a win by two baskets. An entry fee of $100 is charged each team. Over a hundred teams can be expected in the initial year of the tournament, significantly more in later years. Numerous donated awards and trophies are presented in the different divisions. Numerous corporate and business sponsors are solicited to help defray expenses.

SCHEDULING: The tournament is scheduled during the summer months. Competition will last approximately three weeks.

RESOURCES:

Facilities: Games are scheduled in the area's recreation centers, outdoor courts at various parks as well as at the local junior and senior high schools. The championship rounds in each division should be held at a facility that can accommodate a large number of spectators.

Equipment and supplies: Flyers, posters, signs, entry forms, whistles, basketball, and scorebooks are necessary. Portable scoreboards are needed for the championship round of each division.

Publicity and promotion: Extensive advance publicity is needed to insure that potential participants and the general public are aware of this exciting community tournament. Community newspapers and penny-savers can be approached to carry entry forms at reduced costs due to the non-profit nature of this fund raising event. Radio and television stations can provide additional publicity through their coverage of the actual tournament activities, especially the championship games. Entry forms and information sheets should be sent to area schools, health clubs, businesses, etc. Posters can also be displayed throughout the community by businesses and organizations. Announcements should be made at other community events sponsored by the organizers of the three-on-three tournament. Publicize the fact that this is a worthy fund raising activity and specify, at least in general terms, how the profits will be put to use in the community.

Time: Initial plans for the tournament can be organized within a 3-4 week period. Plan 6-9 months in advance when attempting to make reservations for the indoor and outdoor courts needed for the tournament. Plan for 6-8 weeks of advertisements and announcements within the community and another 4-6 weeks for the contestants to send in their entry forms. The tournament can take three weeks with games played evenings and on weekends.

Expenditures: A key ingredient to the success of this tournament is securing corporate sponsors, businesses which will provide money, goods, services and even volunteers in exchange for their names being associated with this community-based event. The use of the game sites and the equipment items and supplies should be gratis. Plan on spending $500 seed money on promotional and publicity efforts.

Personnel (Staff/Volunteers): Numerous volunteers (50-60) and staff (5-7) are needed to plan and organize this event. Some of these volunteers will serve as site supervisors. A few will function as game officials, as needed. However, some organizers do not use game officials until the final championship round in each division. Rather, players in the games "call" their own fouls—on the honor system.

RISK MANAGEMENT: It is absolutely imperative that the entry forms be completed accurately and honestly by the potential contestants as the structure of the tournament is based upon this information. Fair and equitable competition is the objective. Organizers would not want "ringers" (former NCAA division I stars) sneaking onto a team playing within the "high school" division. Entry forms need to have several statements confirming that: (1) contestants will be disqualified for falsified information on the entry forms and (2) contestants hold harmless and release the organizers, volunteers and the sponsoring organization from all liability, damages or responsibility for personal injuries, property damages and other damages whatsoever which may arise from a person's participation in the tournament. Additionally, players under the legal age of 18 must have written signature/permission from their parents or guardians before competing. Financial risks are considerably reduced if local businesses and organizations are obtained as official sponsors of the tournament.

PERMITS/LICENSES: Permission must be secured well in advance to reserve the various basketball courts during the two weeks of the tournament.

HINTS: When players have difficulty calling fouls on themselves in the competition and significant controversy results, organizers need to be ready to provide officials. At the conclusion of the tournament a special ceremony awards prizes and honors to the individual contestants and teams in the various divisions.

Fund raiser #62
Adult Athletic Walk

POTENTIAL NET INCOME: $12,000

COMPLEXITY/DEGREE OF DIFFICULTY: High

DESCRIPTION: Adult supporters and fans of a sport or recreation organization are asked to participate by physically walking a specified number of miles over a predetermined course and by seeking pledges from others, based upon the number of miles. The length of the course could be anywhere from 5-10 miles. Contributors are asked to pledge whatever they care to give for each mile walked. The initial goal should be to obtain 300-500 individuals and/or businesses willing to pledge a donation. If 400 such pledges (averaging just $30) are made, the profit approaches $12,000.

SCHEDULING: The actual "walk" should be scheduled for a Saturday or Sunday afternoon when excellent weather is expected. A rain date, in case of inclement weather, should be advertised well in advance.

RESOURCES:

Facilities: An outdoor course needs to be marked off. The length of the course can vary from 5 miles to 10 miles.

Equipment and supplies: Small and portable tents, prizes (ribbons), tables, chairs, first aid equipment/supplies, portable water coolers/dispensers, signs (both to fit in windows of businesses and larger ones to be stationed throughout the course of the walking route), flyers, posters, portable PA system, safety pins and numbered cloth squares to attached to the back of each walker, and portable restrooms are all necessary items. Donated T-shirts are given to each participant and volunteer helper.

Publicity and promotion: Local businesses and organizations should be asked to display signs and posters. Flyers should be put on windshields of vehicles parked in area malls and shopping centers. The local news media should provide adequate coverage as part of their public service contribution to the community. Announcements should also be made at other public events. Always publicize how the profit made from this fund raiser will be put to good use within the community.

Time: The "walk" can be organized within a week. However, allow 3-4 weeks for the solicitation of pledges and 2-3 days to collect the money following the event. The actual "walk" can take up an entire day (morning till late afternoon). Usually, the "walk" starts around 10 a.m. and concludes sometime in the afternoon.

Expenditures: Attempt to secure most equipment and supplies on a donated or free loan basis. For those items that might have to be purchased, allocate $150. Also, plan on spending up to $250 for promotional and publicity efforts.

Personnel (Staff/Volunteers): Fans, boosters and other volunteers (50-75) as well as staff (3-4) are needed to seek pledges and to participate as "walkers." Additional volunteers (10-15) are also needed to help out on the race course, to assist at starting and finish lines, to provide water to the participants at various points along the course, and to serve as medical personnel.

RISK MANAGEMENT: The greatest danger is having a walker become ill or injured during the walk. To prevent this, volunteer medical personnel should be on hand and there should be frequent rest stops with water available. Don't forget to emphasize that this is a walking experience, not a race. It is a time of solidarity when participants can leisurely walk and enjoy themselves while visiting with other individuals—all for a good cause. Remember that it is not unusual that 10%-15% of the pledges will not result in actual contributions.

PERMITS/LICENSES: Be sure to clear the route with the local police, especially if it crosses any public streets. Also, obtain permission to distribute flyers or handbills on the parking lots of malls and shopping centers.

HINTS: It is helpful to create a course that is pleasant to walk over. Towards this end, organizers frequently attempt to create a course that travels through woods or other pleasant geographical areas. After all, it is a leisurely walk and not a competitive race. Prizes (ribbons and badges) are given to all participants who finish. When seeking pledges, do not forget to approach businesses and organizations within the community, especially those which have some connection with the sponsoring organization. Be sure to remove all signs that are erected over the walking course at the end of the event.

Fund raiser #63
Booster Organization Memberships

POTENTIAL NET INCOME: $12,000 annually

COMPLEXITY/DEGREE OF DIFFICULTY: Moderate

DESCRIPTION: A booster club is organized to provide a source of financial and moral support for the sport or recreation organization. Annual income is generated from various levels or categories of memberships. Each membership category involves a different cost with the more expensive categories providing more benefits (both tangible and intangible). With 250 initial members in the booster entity, averaging just $50 in dues, the net will be close to $12,000.

SCHEDULING: The support group or booster club may be created at any time. However, common sense dictates that the initiation of such a support entity should coincide with when the sport or recreation organization is doing well.

RESOURCES:

Facilities: It is convenient to have use of a room in which meetings may be held, plans organized and phone calls made.

Equipment and supplies: Use of a computer, a laser printer and word processing software will be most helpful in creating a constitution and/or by-laws. Stamps, envelopes and stationery are also necessary, and use of a phone and answering machine.

Publicity and promotion: Individual word of mouth communication is initially utilized. Influential persons should support the parent organization. After the draft governance document(s) is prepared, public announcements should inform fans, supporters and the general public and solicit additional help and input. Announcements and interviews should be featured in the area news media as well as in publications by the organization itself. Similarly, announcements may be made over the PA system and notices displayed on bulletin boards at athletic contests or other gatherings. Once the support group is "off and running" and memberships are being solicited, promoters should emphasize that initial booster members will become "charter members," entitling them to receive nicely crafted and embossed certificates, suitable for framing.

Time: Initial meetings to discuss the formation or creation of a support or booster group should be limited to 60 or 90 minutes. There is always a danger of having meetings that are entirely too long.

Expenditures: There is very little financial outlay in the creation of a support group. Use of meeting rooms or office space as well as equipment such as phones, a computer, printer and software, etc., should be secured on a free or loan basis. The only significant costs will be in the creation (printing/binding) of copies of the formal governance document. Allocate $50 for 200 copies, one copy for each new member. Plan on spending another $50 for 200 copies of impressive certificates to be given to the "charter members," those who join the first year.

Personnel (Staff/Volunteers): A hard core group (10-15) of dedicated and devoted supporters (both volunteers and staff) of the sport or recreation organization should initially work to get the organizational structure of the booster club off the ground in terms of a proposed governance document (constitution and/or by-laws).

RISK MANAGEMENT: There are two major risks involved in the creation of any support group. First, the governance document designed to provide ways the support entity shall operate will not be up to the task for any number of reasons. As a result, much consternation and negative consequences can take place in subsequent years. That is why it is extremely important to have a well-thought-out, clearly written and easily understood governance document. Second, there is always a danger that some individuals and/or constituencies will feel left out of the planning and organizing process. People like to have a say in how things are going to be. To prevent this, planners should provide for one or more open forums during which individuals, groups and organizations will be invited (in a public setting) for input into the working governance document before it is put to a final vote of the members.

PERMITS/LICENSES: None.

HINTS: It is essential not to get too many individuals involved in the detail work of creating the sample or proposed governance document. At this stage in the birth of the support group, less is better. "Too many cooks" do indeed "spoil the pot." It is better to have a smaller group of experienced and skilled individuals work out details such as the purposes, organizational structure and proposed authorized activities and responsibilities of a new support group prior to submitting the working document to a larger group of individuals and organizations for final approval.

Fund raiser #64
Baseball Marathon (100 Innings)

POTENTIAL NET INCOME: $15,000

COMPLEXITY/DEGREE OF DIFFICULTY: High

DESCRIPTION: High school varsity and sub-varsity baseball players are combined and then evenly divided into two teams to compete in a baseball marathon game (100 innings) held as a fund raiser. Profit is derived from (1) pledges solicited in advance from parents, fans, boosters and members of the general community, (2) the sale of admission tickets and (3) a well-run concession. If only 500 pledges (averaging $25) are received, the profit is $12,500. Adding admission and concession profits, the net total can easily reach $15,000.

SCHEDULING: The marathon baseball game is scheduled for a Friday afternoon and runs continuously throughout the evening and night well into Saturday.

RESOURCES:

Facilities: A regulation baseball site with field lights and adequate stands for spectators is needed. Also, an area for a concession stand is highly recommended. Of course, safe parking is a must.

Equipment and supplies: Balls, bats, bases and other normal baseball items of equipment and supplies are required. Additionally, pledge cards, signs, flyers, posters and cash boxes must be secured.

Publicity and promotion: It is imperative that "everyone" in the community become aware of this big fund raising event. Press releases and announcements should appear in area newspapers. Radio and TV stations should provide publicity as part of their public service programs. Local businesses should display signs and posters. And team members and volunteers can distribute flyers throughout the community, including on windshields of parked cars at area malls and shopping centers. There should be a large, highly visible sign at the site of the game. Promote how the profits will be used.

Time: This fund raiser can be organized within a week. However, the solicitation of pledges should be scheduled over a 3-4 week period. Following the 100-inning baseball game the actual cash donations should be collected over a weekend—don't drag the collection process out more than two days.

Expenditures: Plan on spending $200 for publicity and promotional efforts, including pledge cards, signs, posters and flyers. The concession stand can be opened with $250 worth of merchandise. Don't forget to have adequate change on hand for both concessions ($200) and the ticket booth ($100). Everything else should be secured on a free loan or donated basis due to the non-profit nature of the sponsoring organization and the worthy cause.

Personnel (Staff/Volunteers): Players (45), parents (60), volunteers (25) and staff (3) work together to solicit pledges from potential contributors based upon the number of innings to be played. Also, adult volunteers and parents will be organized into teams assigned, on a rotating basis (on 3-4 hour shifts), to staff the concession stand; supervising the parking area; serving as security personnel; and, operating the ticket booth. Volunteers also serve as umpires, announcers, statisticians and scoreboard operators.

RISK MANAGEMENT: A rain date must be publicized. There is no downside financial risk since the marathon will be held regardless of the amount of pledges generated. It is important to have medical personnel available in case of injury or accident. Also, coaches need to avoid letting players become overly tired as a result of participating in the 100-inning marathon and become susceptible to injuries or illness. To prevent this the players must be periodically rotated (open substitutions allowed) into their respective lineups and allowed to rest when they are not playing. Also, no player may pitch more than 9 innings.

PERMITS/LICENSES: The organizers might be required to secure a food concession license. Check with the town clerk or the local health department. Since this fund raiser requires that the baseball lights be on all night, they may be disturbing to nearby residents. It may be necessary to obtain formal permission from community leaders. Finally, check to see if you need permission to place flyers on the windshields of vehicles parked at malls and shopping centers.

HINTS: Expect 10%-15% of the money pledged to be non-collectable, for any number of reasons. This is to be expected when dealing with pledges. This fund raiser can easily become an annual happening. Instead of soliciting pledges based on the number of innings to be played, organizers can procure pledges based on the number of strike outs, or the number of home runs or the number of runs scored by both teams. This fund raiser can also be organized around a "cash up front" concept rather than the "pledge concept." In this scenario, contributions are actually collected prior to the game based on the fact that 100 innings will be played. For example, contributors would donate from ten cents to $1 (or more) for each inning to be played. This eliminates the time-consuming task of having to contact contributors twice–first to solicit the pledge and the second time to actually collect the money.

Fund raiser #65
Doughnuts and Other Pastry
Items for Sale

POTENTIAL NET INCOME: $15,000 Annually

COMPLEXITY/DEGREE OF DIFFICULTY: Moderate

DESCRIPTION: Doughnuts and other types of pastry are sold before, during and after school hours throughout the academic year. The pastry items are obtained on a wholesale basis from a local bakery and sold by student-athlete volunteers at selected sites throughout the school.

SCHEDULING: This fund raising activity takes place on each school day within the school. The food can also be sold inside or outside the building(s) before and after school as well as during so-called free periods. Typically, coaches and their athletes in a specific sport are given the opportunity to run the "pastry operation" during their season with the proceeds going directly to their sport budget. When a new season rolls around, athletes (and their coaches) in a different sport are given the opportunity to try.

RESOURCES:

Facilities: If school authorities permit the pastry to be sold in the facility, the student sellers can set up at a table almost anywhere—in the cafeteria, in a specific classroom or even in the hallway. The students work in twos or threes and sell the pastries right out of the boxes in which they were picked up fresh from the bakery.

Equipment and supplies: Having portable tables or display areas helps to motivate students, faculty and administrators to buy the items. A cash box, $30 in change, a receipt and record book are also needed.

Publicity and promotion: Special promotions should be held for each of the holiday seasons with appropriately colored icing on the pastry. Word-of-mouth will form the best advertising. Announcements over the school public address system will also help publicize the availability of the goodies and the purpose for which the profits will be used. The items are promoted on the basis of their freshness, their excellent taste and the fact that the profits will go to a good cause, that is, the students' own athletic program.

Time: It takes approximately 30 to 45 minutes extra work in the morning to stop at the local bakery and then to get set up for the morning foot traffic. Similarly, the accounting of the money later that afternoon will consume some 20 minutes and will involve the student sellers and the supervising coach or sponsor. Planning for the ongoing fund raising event can be completed within a week.

Expenditures: The principal cost for this effort is the cost of goods, that is, the baked goods. $50 should purchase a beginning inventory of pastries.

Personnel (Staff/Volunteers): 20 or so volunteers (students and coaches) can effectively run this program during a sport season.

RISK MANAGEMENT: Health and sanitary matters should remain of prime concern to the students and their coaches/sponsors. Sellers must wear plastic gloves and be neat in appearance. Also, they are not allowed to eat or drink anything while involved in selling the food. The pastry itself must be truly attractive and delicious or fickle students will not be repeat customers. Strict financial accounting is required in order to prevent any perception of misuse of monies. It is imperative that the bakery be paid on time with an approved check each week.

PERMITS/LICENSES: Selling the pastry on school property usually does not entail the securing of a permit or a license. However, some locals have ordinances prohibiting such sales and would-be promoters need to check with their local municipal licensing board to ascertain the legality.

HINTS: This type of fund raising activity is more successful if there are no vending machines selling similar items within the school. The fund raising project does not involve the selling of drinks as there are usually vending machines available for them. Be sure that the facility is not littered with debris as a result of careless or messy customers. Towards this end it is necessary that those individuals selling the food also police their physical site so that school officials don't complain about untidiness. The hardest part of this project may very well be receiving initial permission from the school authorities to sell the goodies on school property.

Fund raiser #66
Home for the Holidays

POTENTIAL NET INCOME: $15,000

COMPLEXITY/DEGREE OF DIFFICULTY: High

DESCRIPTION: In the spirit of Christmas, a spacious and elegant "showcase home" or mansion (15 to 20 rooms), capable of accommodating large crowds, is selected as the *"Home for the Holidays."* The mansion will become a beautifully decorated open house exhibiting magnificent and charming displays of holiday decorations. In fact, each room is decorated in a different theme. Various corporate sponsors help to re-create an authentic early colonial dining room, including period decorations such as gingerbread houses and floral and fruit displays and accessories. Additionally, one or more chefs will hold cooking demonstrations and will offer samples to the touring guests. Visitors, who pay $12 at the door and $10 for advance tickets, will find holiday ideas galore while meandering through the mansion. Gourmet sandwiches and specialty drinks may be purchased. Additional profits are realized through the sale of a variety of tasteful and unique holiday gifts (for Christmas, Halloween, Thanksgiving and New Years) in the "boutique," which is created in one of the mansion's downstairs rooms. Many of the items used to decorate the rooms are for sale in the "boutique."

SCHEDULING: The open house is scheduled during December.

RESOURCES:

Facilities: A showcase home or mansion is needed where visitors may enjoy a Yuletide experience reminiscent of holiday get-togethers of the past. Private owners of such homes or historical societies may be approached to secure permission to use such sites.

Equipment and supplies: Decorations, trees, flowers, food, drink, cooking utensils, paper plates, cups, napkins, spoons, prizes and awards, signs, posters, markers, cash boxes, receipt and record books, tickets, tables and chairs as well as plastic runners for the rugs are all required. Items for sale must also be on hand.

Publicity and promotion: Newspapers and penny-savers should run feature articles as well as provide other types of coverage for this non-profit, community based fund raising effort. Radio and television stations may provide free exposure and publicity through their Public Service Announcements (PSAs). Businesses and organizations can display signs and posters promoting the *"Home for the Holidays"* while some can sell advance tickets. Of course, the corporate sponsors play a big role in helping to publicize the *"Home for the Holidays"* in their own publications and in-store promotions. Continually promote this event as a non-profit fund raising effort sponsored by a community based organization. Also, publicize how the profits will be spent.

Time: It will take three to four weeks to plan and organize this complicated fund raising project. Identifying a suitable mansion and securing permission to use it can take six to nine months. Lining up the corporate sponsors and other volunteers can take from four to eight weeks. The makeover of the home is to be done within 48 hours. The decorated *"Home for the Holidays"* is open for a two week period before Christmas from 10 a.m. to 8 p.m. Plan to spend at least a day to restore the site to its original condition.

Expenditures: The use of the mansion should be obtained on a gratis basis due to the non-profit nature of the fund raising group and the worthy cause for which the profits will be spent. However, if the mansion belongs to an organization such as the local historical society and a rental fee is absolutely necessary, this cost can be offset by contributions from one or more sponsors. Or, a sharing of the profits can be negotiated. $1,500 in seed money is needed, mostly for advertisements and publicity efforts.

Personnel (Staff/Volunteers): A large number of volunteers and staff (50-75) are needed to sell and take tickets, solicit corporate and individual sponsors, secure donated decorations, food, to serve as hosts/hostesses, and members of decorating and clean-up teams. It is imperative that "heavy hitters" or important centers of influence within the community "get on board" early in the planning process since these individuals are invaluable in convincing others (individuals and businesses) to become involved in this fund raiser.

RISK MANAGEMENT: To prevent theft or damage to the home, volunteers should always be visibly present throughout the home when it is open to the public. Financial risk is significantly reduced with the solicitation of corporate sponsors. To protect the carpeting, plastic runners are placed on the floor where the patrons are expected to walk.

PERMITS/LICENSES: None.

HINTS: If the site is a private mansion, the owners must agree to physically leave while their home is open to the public. In some instances the owners might be traveling for the holidays and thus will not be too inconvenienced. In other instances, the owners must be accommodated in a fine hotel for the 16-day duration. Thus, it is helpful to secure a first class hotel as a corporate sponsor. This sponsor's contribution is free use of a suite (with meals) for the 16 days and nights.

Fund raiser #67
Musical Concert

POTENTIAL NET INCOME: $15,000

COMPLEXITY/DEGREE OF DIFFICULTY: High

DESCRIPTION: The sport or recreation organization contracts with a popular musical group, through an agent, to conduct a one-night concert. Tickets for the affair will be priced based at what the market will bear for the visiting musical group, the cost of the group, and the fact that $15,000 net profit is desired by the sponsoring organization. Profits will be generated from the sale of advance tickets, on site tickets plus food concessions. Be aware that some sites have stipulations that all food concession profits remain with the owner(s) of the site itself. The musical group will almost always retain the financial profits from the sale of all music paraphernalia associated with their group that is sold by their staff at the concert.

SCHEDULING: The concert is scheduled on a Friday or Saturday evening.

RESOURCES:

Facilities: A large municipal or educational facility (indoor or outdoor) large enough to allow upwards of 10,000 people to attend. In some locales the musical group can perform on a football field with spectators in the stands. Adequate and safe parking is required. It is imperative that the physical surroundings be able to be secured by authorities to prevent disruptive behavior before, during or after the concert. The touring musicians will have minimum requirements for any site.

Equipment and supplies: Displays, posters, signs, flyers, tickets, and cash boxes must be obtained. If concessions are to be the responsibility of the sponsoring organization then all food concession equipment, supplies and inventory must be obtained.

Publicity and promotion: Effective advance publicity is the key to this fund raiser. Repeated announcements in the area media are a must. Trade-outs with the media for concert tickets are expected. Also, signs and posters should be displayed in numerous businesses in the surrounding communities. Some of the businesses can also serve as ticket outlets. Contracting with a ticket service will insure the best possible advance ticket sales. The cost of $2-$4 per ticket is well worth the service provided.

Time: This fund raiser is a very time intensive project to plan, organize and implement. Planning for the event can take 4-8 weeks. In many instances arrangements with popular groups must be made through their agents 6-8-10 months in advance or longer. The concert usually lasts three hours or so. Cleanup can take 3-4 hours.

Expenditures: The two largest areas of cash outlays will be for the musical group itself and the rental of the site where the concert will be held. A third large area of expense includes promotional and publicity expenses including payments of a percentage to a ticket service. The downside financial risk (commitment) can run as high as $50,000.

Personnel (Staff/Volunteers): Off-duty police officers must be hired to work the concert to augment the municipal officers assigned to the event. A large number of volunteers (35-50) and staff (2-5) are needed to help market and publicize the concert to the general public. Volunteers (50) can also be used as ushers and food concession operators. If the site is a municipal facility there may be a requirement that regular municipal workers be used to work the concert.

RISK MANAGEMENT: There is a very real financial risk in this type of fund raiser. First, there is always the possibility that insufficient fans will pay to hear the group perform. In all cases, the musical group will insist that a major portion of their payment be paid in advance or held in escrow by a bank until the concert is completed. Insufficient paid attendance is no excuse for not paying the group. Second, there is always the danger of violence at some musical concerts. Extreme care must be taken to insure that this risk be minimized by working closely with police, public safety, and health authorities.

PERMITS/LICENSES: In many communities a special use permit must be secured prior to holding any type of large concert.

HINTS: Secure the services of the most popular singing group for the community where the concert will be held. It is foolish to book an expensive rock and roll group if the general public is more interested in country and western music. Don't scrimp on the cost of the musical group. Secure the best, most popular group you can. Cooperate with local authorities in terms of providing the safest facility and concert possible. Almost every musical group will present a written list of requirements that they insist upon being met by the sponsoring entity. Some of these requirements pertain to the type of airline transportation to the city where the concert is to be held (first class); the transportation provided from the airport to the hotel (limousine); the quality of the hotel the group will be staying at (the very highest); and, the type of refreshments provided within the hotel room (extensive list of food and drink), etc. Work with the agent(s) of the musical group to determine exactly what the group expects and what the sponsoring group can expect in return.

Fund raiser #68
Endowment Challenge

POTENTIAL NET INCOME: $16,000 each year

COMPLEXITY/DEGREE OF DIFFICULTY: High

DESCRIPTION: Cash contributions are solicited from individuals and businesses to go into an endowment fund, which can be established by any organization which has raised a large sum of money and elects to spend only the proceeds from the interest generated while retaining the principal. The amount of money in an endowment can range anywhere from $10,000 to $1 million or more. The principal sum is never touched, i.e., spent. Rather, it remains in some type of interest-bearing account, usually in perpetuity. It is the interest generated annually from the principal sum which provides income for the program each year. It is generally considered necessary to generate at least $10,000 as a minimum amount for an endowment fund in order to make it a worthwhile effort. If a specific endowment contains some $200,000 and is safely invested at 8% interest the sponsoring organization will generate $16,000 for each year that the principal sum is invested at this rate of interest. Contributions to an endowment fund can be generated through any number of ways—not the least of which, and perhaps still the most effective, is simply to ask for donations to the fund.

SCHEDULING: Planning for the endowment challenge can be completed within 3-4 weeks. Solicitation efforts for money can be initiated any time. Once established, contributions can continue to be solicited on an ongoing basis to increase the endowment and therefore the interest earned by the organization each year. An endowment fund may be established by a sport or recreation organization in the name of some noted individual (living or deceased) who worked in that specific organization. For example, a well-respected coach, athlete or administrator. Hence, the endowment would be called the Clark Whited Endowment Fund and all of the players, coaches and fans of Clark Whited (as well as the general public) would be potential donors to the fund. The interest would be spent annually for any significant purpose for which the endowment fund had been originally established. An endowment should never be established to spend money on something like utilities, postage or office supplies. An endowment fund could also be created and named for the purpose for which money from the endowment will be spent, that is, the Camp Endowment Fund for Disadvantaged Youths.

RESOURCES:

Facilities: None.

Equipment and supplies: Record books, stationery, envelopes, stamps and a photo plaque are all necessary.

Publicity and promotion: Extensive person-to-person communication and solicitation is a must in this type of fund raising effort. Similarly, periodic mail and/or phone campaigns to targeted individuals should be implemented. Extensive free publicity can be obtained from the media both when the endowment is established and when significant contributions are received or when specific monetary levels are reached.

Time: Although there are no time limitations or requirements in this type of fund raiser, it is suggested that the minimal goal required to establish the endowment be achieved within a 6-8 week period. Then, when this minimum amount ($10,000 for example) has been raised the sponsoring group can publicly announce the great achievement while continuing to seek additional contributions as time passes.

Expenditures: Expenditures will principally revolve around telephone and mailing expenses plus any printed materials (brochures or flyers) created. Plan on spending up to $300 for seed money.

Personnel (Staff/Volunteers): Volunteers (15-20) and staff (3-5) form the nucleus of the sales force who attempt to sell the idea or concept of contributing to an endowment fund. The services and advice of a competent attorney and/or accountant should be sought regarding legal and financial matters.

RISK MANAGEMENT: There are no significant risks involved in solicitation of funds for the endowment. There are some risks, however, once money is collected. It is prudent, therefore, to check with competent professionals in terms of (1) of the legal ramifications associated with the establishment and maintenance of an endowment fund, and (2) where to keep the principal sum of money that has been raised. Similarly, there is always a risk in terms of how to invest the principal. Should it be invested in stocks? Should it be placed in a certificate of deposit (CD) in a local bank? Who shall be responsible for determining where the money shall be invested? Should a single individual be given this responsibility or should a committee?

PERMITS/LICENSES: None

HINTS: Once such an endowment fund has been created, it is prudent to publicize such by displaying a photo plaque conspicuously in the recreation or sport facility so that the general public visiting the facility will become aware of the existence of the endowment fund and its purpose(s). This enhances the image of the sponsoring organization and opens the doors for future contributions.

Fund raiser #69
Coeducational Invitational
Track Extravaganza

POTENTIAL NET INCOME: $17,000

COMPLEXITY/DEGREE OF DIFFICULTY: High

DESCRIPTION: An area or statewide coeducational track meet for senior high schools and colleges is sponsored by a sport or recreational organization. The meet provides competition for high schools to compete against other secondary schools and college athletes to compete against other collegiate athletes. Plan for a total of 20 schools to participate. Profit to the sponsoring organization is derived from contributions obtained from area businesses and organizations ($10,000), entry fees ($200 each team), sale of admission tickets ($3,000), and sale of concession ($1,500) and apparel ($500) items.

SCHEDULING: The invitational meet is scheduled in the spring and is a two-day event, Friday and Saturday. Be sure to check for possible conflicts with other track meets on the same date. Try to stay away from other large track meets scheduled in your area of the state for the same date.

RESOURCES:

Facilities: A regulation track facility is essential. Adequate seating (2,000 to 3,000) for spectators is highly desirable as is suitable parking. Lights for nighttime competition are required.

Equipment and supplies: All of the normal equipment and supplies required to conduct any track meet must be on hand. All items should be in excellent condition. Similarly, concession inventory and apparel (T- shirts, hats, etc.) must also be purchased. Numerous individual and team awards should be secured, hopefully on a donated basis.

Publicity and promotion: The track meet is billed (promoted) as the "biggest combined secondary/collegiate invitational track extravaganza" in the area or state. Business leaders should be approached for contributions on the basis of helping the sponsoring group, a deserving non-profit entity, and also helping to promote the community itself. After all, with some 20 teams (1200 athletes) and many, many parents involved in the competition, the financial and public relations impact to the community is significant.

Time: Planning for this size event will take several (3-4) weeks. It will take even longer (6-8 months) to line up a sufficient number of teams to be involved in the initial track meet. The facility needs to be reserved at the earliest possible date. The selling of advance tickets can take place over a period of 2-3 weeks. However, most tickets will be sold on site. To set up the facility for the track and field events and for the concession/apparel booths will require at least a half-day of preparation. The meet will start on Friday at 2 p.m. and will run until 10 p.m. that night. The meet will continue early next morning (8 a.m.) and conclude late that evening.

Expenditures: Allocate $1,000 for seed money. Promotional and publicity costs, including stamps, stationery and phone expenses, will be around $400. Beginning inventory for concessions and apparel can initially total $400 and $200 respectfully. Budget $500 for meet officials if they cannot be secured on a donated basis. Awards, if not donated, will cost $500.

Personnel (Staff/Volunteers): The success of this fund raising project rests in securing sufficient volunteers willing to help out in this involved and very hectic fund raising project. Fans, supporters and members of the sponsoring group (30-45) can play a big role in not only helping to publicize and promote this event but also in soliciting contributions from businesses and organizations. Additional volunteers and helpers (30) will be needed to serve as officials, statisticians, ticket sellers, publicists, concessionaires, and on-site supervisors.

RISK MANAGEMENT: Legal liability exposure is reduced to a minimum concerning The concession stand if all health rules and regulations are strictly adhered to. The financial risk is greatly reduced, if not eliminated, with the successful solicitation of contributions from area businesses. Similarly, the entrance fees, nominal as they are, provide protection against any real financial loss.

PERMITS/LICENSES: A license might be necessary to operate the concession stand. Check with the town clerk or health department.

HINTS: Check the state high school athletic association to insure that there is no statewide prohibition against high school athletes competing in a track meet held in conjunction with (but not providing competition against) collegiate athletes. Once this track extravaganza becomes a success the task of inviting schools to participate becomes much easier. In fact, after a few years there will be schools inviting themselves to the event. Of course, this is dependent upon how those teams, individual athletes, and their families are treated who do participate in the early track meets. When initially buying apparel to resell at the meet order hats, T-shirts, etc., without a date on them. Thus, if any items are left over they may be sold the following year. After several years of successfully hosting this event, the apparel items may be expanded to include other types of merchandise and the actual year of the meet can be included.

Fund raiser #70
Taste of the Nations

POTENTIAL NET INCOME: $17,000

COMPLEXITY/DEGREE OF DIFFICULTY: High

DESCRIPTION: A sophisticated wine and dine event, the *"Taste of the Nations"* involves wonderful gourmet goodies (wide range of foods and numerous wines) that literally represent the tastes of the world. Fifteen to 20 restaurants and wineries donate food and drink as well as personnel for the evening. Other community businesses are approached to contribute both cash and goods to make this event a truly memorable one for all involved. Advance tickets are sold to the general public for $35 per person. At the door the tickets are $45 per person. The anticipated number of patrons is between 600 and

800. Additional activities taking place during the evening include a live auction and "mystery envelope prizes" which will be given to lucky ticket holders drawn at random. A popular band will provide music.

SCHEDULING: The event is scheduled on a Saturday evening.

RESOURCES:

Facilities: The wine and dine festivity is held at a major hotel or party house in the community. Adequate and safe parking is a must.

Equipment and supplies: Signs, flyers, posters, decorations, international foods and wines, tables, chairs, tablecloths, eating utensils, a cash box, and receipt/record books area all necessary.

Publicity and promotion: Extensive and numerous public announcements are required to make this fund raising event a huge success. Newspapers and penny-savers should provide free publicity due to the nature of this non-profit fund raising effort. Similarly, radio and television stations should be approached to provide free Public Service Announcements (PSAs). Specialty publications such as the local "Entertainment and Arts Magazine" are ideal sources of feature stories about the organizing group's fund raising efforts. Be sure to publicize a local phone number for more information. Local businesses and organizations can display signs and posters promoting the "Taste of the Nations" fund raiser. Flyers can also be placed on the windshields of vehicles parked at local malls and shopping centers. Finally, use the PA system at other recreation or athletic events sponsored by the organizing group to promote the upcoming *"Taste of the Nations"* fund raiser. Highlight the fact that this is a worthwhile fund raising effort sponsored by a local non-profit organization when soliciting contributions from area businesses and when promoting ticket sales.

Time: Planning for this event will consume 6-8 months, especially if this is the first time for this fund raiser. The ticket selling window should be 4-6 weeks. Allow 4-5 hours to prepare the facility on the day of the event for patrons, including setting up the decorations and displaying the items for the auction and giveaways. The actual event will begin at 6 p.m. and will conclude around 9 p.m. Cleanup will take several hours and will be done by the hotel staff.

Expenditures: This fund raising project can be initiated with $300 in seed money. All other costs can be paid from the proceeds of ticket sales. Organizers should attempt to get almost everything needed for this event donated, loaned or purchased at a deep discount. Initially, the cost of the hotel and the band will most likely have to be paid out of the ticket proceeds. Later, when this fund raiser becomes more accepted and popular, it may be possible to secure use of a class hotel for gratis, or at a greatly reduced price because of the non-profit nature of the organizing group. Similarly, local bands, anxious for increased exposure, may be willing to donate their talent or reduce their price if they know that they will be seen by literally hundreds of influential members of the community. Total expenditures might approach $2,000, including expenses for the hotel and band.

Personnel (Staff/Volunteers): A large number of volunteers (45-50) and staff (2-4) are needed to help plan, organize and implement this fun-packed evening. Helpers are needed to solicit sponsors, donors, sell tickets, run the evening's auction. A professional auctioneer's services (donated) are needed. A popular band must be chosen.

RISK MANAGEMENT: The financial risks are diminished if the donated items and services are secured prior to publicly announcing the kick-off of the ticket sales. There is very limited legal liability exposure involved in this fund raiser since the event is being held in a public hotel and is being professionally catered by various restaurants and their professional staffs.

PERMITS/LICENSES: The host hotel will possess all of the necessary licenses and permits. Thus, no special food permits or liquor licenses are needed. Prior permission must be secured from the malls and shopping centers before distributing flyers on vehicles in their parking lots.

HINTS: This fund raiser can easily become an annual event, one that expands both in terms of the number of patrons and the number of companies taking part in the festivities. For subsequent fund raisers, the donating restaurants and wineries will find themselves competing with one another to provide "the best possible feast" for the patrons, thus elevating the quality of the evening considerably. Similarly, there will be other businesses willing to jump on the highly successful "bandwagon" and contribute even more goods, services and money—all for a worthy cause.

Fund raiser #71
Vehicle Donation

POTENTIAL NET INCOME: $20,000

COMPLEXITY/DEGREE OF DIFFICULTY: Low

DESCRIPTION: A legally designated "not-for-profit" sport or recreation organization seeks donations of used vehicles (cars, trucks, boats, trailers, motorhomes and RVs) from individuals. The donated vehicles can be utilized in three ways. First, they may be used in the normal course of business by the non-profit group. Second, they may be bartered for other much needed items of equipment or supplies, And, third, the donated items may be sold for much needed cash.

SCHEDULING: This fund raising tactic can be an ongoing effort throughout the calendar year.

RESOURCES:

Facilities: A site is needed where the donated vehicles can be temporarily and safely stored until they can be disposed of appropriately. Some vehicles may be stored at individual supporters' homes or businesses.

Equipment and supplies: Posters, signs, and receipt books are all that are necessary.

Publicity and promotion: The general public must be made aware of the effort to accept donated vehicles in exchange for the possibility of securing tax advantages on individual or business tax returns. This can best be accomplished by periodic and consistent advertisements over local radio (and in some instances, television) stations. Use a catchy slogan in the advertisements. The goal is to make the general public aware that such donations can significantly help a worthy, local, non-profit group and that there may be positive tax benefits for donors. The area newspapers and penny-savers can also include mention of the "vehicle donation" program. In some instances, these advertisements can be obtained at a reduced cost or even on a free basis because of the non-profit nature of the fund raising effort. Public announcements over the PA system should also be made at various sport contests or recreation events sponsored by the same organization.

Time: Planning and organizing this project can be completed within a week. The solicitation of vehicle donations should be an ongoing process throughout the year.

Expenditures: Plan on budgeting $1,000 for advertising costs to get this fund raising project off the ground.

Personnel (Staff/Volunteers): A small number of volunteers (2-3) and staff (1-2) can successfully plan, organize and implement the vehicle donation program. Other helpers (5-10) are needed to make some selected repairs on the vehicles as needed. And still others (5-7) are needed to help dispose of the donated vehicles in the most efficient and profitable manner possible.

RISK MANAGEMENT: The downside financial risk is the sum allocated for the initial radio and newspaper advertisements. The legal exposure is minimal as long as no tax or legal advice is given by representatives of the sponsoring/soliciting organization to donors.

PERMITS/LICENSES: This fund raising effort is dependent upon the soliciting organization being qualified under the current IRS code as a not-for-profit organization. Donations to such organizations enable the donors to claim a tax deduction on the then current fair market value of the item(s) donated.

HINTS: It is imperative that neither the organization accepting the donations nor its representatives become involved in assessing the value of the gift for the donor. Rather, the donor has the responsibility of securing an accurate estimate of the item's value. The receiving organization merely provides a receipt indicating the date of the gift transaction and identifying the donated object, not the value of the object. Donors should be encouraged to check with their accountants or tax attorneys to determine actual tax consequences for any sizeable donation. Finally, those vehicles that cannot be put to good use by the organization need to be quickly disposed of, preferably sold for cash and the cash put to good use.

Fund raiser #72
National Alumni(ae) Tennis Tournaments

POTENTIAL NET INCOME: $20,000

COMPLEXITY/DEGREE OF DIFFICULTY: Moderate

DESCRIPTION: Selected alumni of a school or past associates of an sport or recreation organization are contacted via phone and asked to conduct a fund raising tennis tournament in their own communities on behalf of the parent organization. All of the tournaments, held throughout the country, are scheduled for the same weekend, if at all possible. Income is derived from entrance fees, sponsorships and the selling of advertisements at each site. The profits from each tournament, gross income minus the costs of conducting each tournament, are sent to the parent entity. If 20 different tournaments are held at different locations in the country and if an average of only $1,000 profit is realized at each site, the parent organization will still receive $20,000 in net profit.

SCHEDULING: The tennis tournaments may be scheduled during the spring, summer or fall months. The individual tournaments will take place on a Friday, Saturday and Sunday. Individual needs and limitations may necessitate some variance from this schedule.

RESOURCES:

Facilities: The competition could be held at public courts, at a school site, or at a private or public country a tennis club.

Equipment and supplies: All items of equipment and supplies are to be obtained by the local volunteers at each site throughout the country. Donated prizes, balls, posters, signs and decorations are the responsibility of the local organizers.

Publicity and promotion: The parent organization should prepare and send (1) a package of tournament ideas and suggestions as well as (2) sample press releases to the various organizing committees or tournament directors. The unique nature of these tennis tournaments as well as the non-profit nature of the parent organization are highlighted in all publicity materials. Local organizing committees might consider announcements in local newspapers and penny-savers as well as over the radio and television airwaves. Local businesses and organizations might display signs and posters promoting the tournament.

Time: This project can be planned and organized in 2-3 weeks. The courts should be reserved as early as possible to eliminate any possibility of a scheduling conflict. It may take as long as 2-3 months however to line up the various local tournament directors and committees. It may take 3-5 weeks or even longer for the local tournament directors throughout the country to establish the tournament committees and to actually organize the local tournaments. For example, courts must be reserved, publicity and promotional campaigns must be planned and implemented, contestants signed up, sponsors solicited and donations obtained.

Expenditures: The expenses for the parent organizations involve phone usage, stamps and copying costs. However, even these costs can be minimized or eliminated entirely if local individuals or businesses will allow free use of their phones and copy machines and contribute the postage necessary to complete the mailings. Prizes for the local tournaments are secured on a donated basis in the local communities as are other equipment and supplies. Thus, total downside financial exposure is limited to less than $300.

Personnel (Staff/Volunteers): Important centers of influence (influential, important people) from the parent organization are needed to personally contact loyal and supportive alumni and friends of the organization to solicit their assistance in running these tennis tournaments in their own hometowns. The key to the success of this fund raising concept is being able to secure interested and loyal supporters, in different sections of the country, who will assume a true leadership role in planning, organizing and implementing a fund raising sport tournament on behalf of the parent or sponsoring organization.

RISK MANAGEMENT: There is little risk either in terms of finances or legal liability for the parent organization.

PERMITS/LICENSES: There may be a need to secure a permit or make a reservation for the tennis courts at the various local sites.

HINTS: It is important that the local organizing committee or tournament directors be allowed great freedom and discretion in conducting their own tournaments in their own communities. The tasks facing the parent organization include: (1) to find individuals willing to plan and implement such a fund raising effort in their own communities on behalf of the parent organization, (2) to provide guidance and assistance whenever necessary to local organizers, (3) to graciously accept the profits from each site, and (4) to express deep and sincere (public) appreciation to those leaders who made the individual tournaments successful and financially profitable. The concept of simultaneous athletic contests or tournaments taking place at different sites throughout the country can be equally effective with sports other than tennis. For example, tournaments involving basketball, softball, volleyball and baseball could also be used to generate big money for a non- profit parent organization.

Fund raiser #73
Weekly Sports Pool

POTENTIAL NET INCOME: $25,000 annually

COMPLEXITY/DEGREE OF DIFFICULTY: Low

DESCRIPTION: This fund raising project in an on-going sports pool in which at least 200 (hopefully more) booster club members, "friends" or contributors donate $5 each on a weekly basis. From the total weekly pot of $1,000 (for 200 participants), the athletic or recreation program retains 50% while the rest is returned to the winner of the weekly sport pool. The winner is determined by successfully predicting scores (on a game card) of a certain number of area or national athletic contests played during the week, or by predicting total number of points scored in one or more athletic contests. On an annual basis, this fund raiser can generate over $25,000 in net profits.

SCHEDULING: The winners of this sports pool can be announced at periodic contests and/or at bi-weekly or monthly meetings of the athletic program, the youth sport league or the recreation department. Provide the opportunity for participants to write monthly or annual checks. Writing a weekly check can quickly become something of a nuisance and is viewed by many as "more trouble than it is worth." Besides, people tend to forget writing weekly checks.

RESOURCES:

Facilities: No special facilities are required.

Equipment and supplies: Entry forms (game cards), stamps and envelopes are needed as are display posters and signs used in promoting the contests.

Publicity and promotion: Word of mouth coupled with written communication with booster club members, ticket holders or supporters of the sponsoring group can be quite effective. When announcing winners publicly at a contest, meeting or gathering, this is the ideal time to promote additional participation and provide opportunities to sign up new participants for future sport pools in the coming weeks, months and year ahead. Place attractive posters and signs in local businesses publicizing the sports pool as well as announcing the recent winners and the amounts won (perhaps with photos of past winners). Approach the local paper or pennysaver about carrying information about the winners.

Time: The overall structure of this weekly fund raising project can be completed within a week. Determining the weekly winner(s) and structuring the upcoming week's contest or sport pool can be accomplished within 30-45 minutes. Winnings can be distributed (by check) at future meetings or athletic contests of the group or else mailed to the recipients. This is accomplished with a minimum of time.

Expenditures: All prize money is generated from the profits of the sport pool. Other expenditures include entry forms, posters and flyers as well as stamps and envelopes to be used to mail winnings. Plan on spending $1,000 a year on total expenses.

Personnel (Staff/Volunteers): Volunteers (30-35) and staff (2-3) play an important role in getting this fund raising concept off the ground. However, once the "Weekly Sports Pool" is off and running, it is almost self-sufficient except for efforts to gain additional "players" and reduce likelihood of defections. Towards this end, 15-20 individuals, whose responsibility is just that, work on expanding the base of participants and to encourage dropouts from the sports pool to rejoin. Naturally, adult supervision is required in terms of supervising the sports pool, determining the winner(s) of the weekly contest and the distribution of the prize monies (via mail and check).

RISK MANAGEMENT: There is little downside financial risk involved since the prize money is taken from the gross income. Legal liability concerns should be addressed by the umbrella policy carried by the sponsoring group.

PERMITS/LICENSES: Sport pools, being considered games of chance or gambling, are restricted or regulated in many states and many more communities. Local promoters should check with the town clerk or municipal offices to determine appropriate rules and regulations.

HINTS: Establish a definite date each week when the game cards or entry forms and the money must be received to be eligible for that week's sports pool. Also, identify one or more consistent sites where contestants can drop off their money and entry forms. Once this type of fund raising project gets off the ground it can continue for years on end as a successful and popular fund raiser. The reason this project is so popular hinges upon two factors. The first is based upon the significant amount of money generated for the athletic or the recreation program with a minimum of effort. The second is rooted in human nature and has to do with the so-called "gambling itch" and the fact that significant monies can be won by the participants. It is important to personally call or meet in person any previous participant in the sports pool who misses a specific week's contest in an effort to find out what happened. This is also an excellent opportunity to encourage the individual to write a check to cover the next twelve months of the Weekly Sport Pool. Finally, this fund raising project starts with one's own members or boosters or supporters. It then can be expanded to others within the community. The key is to always attempt to expand the base of contributors or "players" thereby expanding the potential profit. Anticipate a dropout rate of some 10% to 15% a year. These players have to be "replaced" on a regular basis.

Fund raiser #74
Celebrity Golf Tournament

POTENTIAL NET INCOME: $26,500 or more

COMPLEXITY/DEGREE OF DIFFICULTY: High

DESCRIPTION: The distinguishing factor of this type of golf tournament is the involvement of local and/or national celebrities playing in the foursomes alongside golfers from the local communities. These celebrities either donate their presence or receive a modest stipend. An evening banquet is also planned. Profits result from the sale of tickets as well as sponsorships and advertisements from area businesses plus "sale" of greens and tees. Tickets for golf, a cart and the evening banquet sell for $150 per person. With an anticipated 150 golfers the gross take is $22,500. With businesses or sponsors paying $500 each for the right to display advertising on each of the eighteen tees and on each of the greens, an additional $18,000 brings the gross income to $40,500.

SCHEDULING: The tournament and banquet is scheduled on a Saturday when the weather is expected to be accommodating. Additionally, there are several roving golf carts continually bringing refreshments (cold drinks and sandwiches) to the golfers out on the course. The tournament usually involves a shotgun start (all tee off same time on different holes) around 9 a.m. and continues throughout the day. With 150 participants this comes to around 2 foursomes per hole. However, another option is to have all foursomes begin from the same tee. Since it takes about eight minutes for a foursome to start, it could take up to 5 hours (beginning at 8 a.m.) for thirty-seven foursomes to tee off resulting in a staggered finish at the end. When the golfers finish the course in the afternoon they may go to the clubhouse (hospitality area) to change clothes, relax, recap their game and watch one of several large screen televisions for the national sports news prior to the banquet. On the golf course itself there are numerous contests at each hole for both men and for women. Some of these contests include (1) closest to the pin, (2) longest drive, (3) longest putt, (4) low gross, (5) low net, etc. At the banquet awards are also given out for the various winners.

RESOURCES:

Facilities: A challenging 18-hole golf course is mandatory along with excellent banquet facilities and suitable parking.

Equipment and supplies: Golf carts, various trophies and a suitable sound system for the banquet are needed. Posters, flyers and signs for the tees and greens must be created. A microphone and good sound system.

Publicity and promotion: The strength of the marketing effort rests in the volunteers who attract and solicit both paying golfers and gain commitment from the celebrities to take part in this non-profit fund raiser. The publicity centers around the numerous celebrities taking part in the tournament, the opportunity to play in an exciting foursome plus an excellent evening banquet. Don't forget to publicize the purpose for which the money raised will be used. Posters and flyers should be displayed in area businesses, some of which could serve as ticket outlets. Free media coverage can be secured when easily recognized celebrities are involved.

Time: A three- to six-month planning period should provide adequate time to properly organize this tournament, to reserve the course and obtain commitments from the celebrities. The golfing activity will consume up to 6 hours while the banquet festivities will take another 2 hours.

Expenditures: Major expenses center around (1) advertising and promotions ($500), (2) stipends for the celebrities ($5,000), (3) rental of the golf course and carts (an average of $30 per person), and (4) banquet costs ($20 per person). Awards should be secured on a donated basis. Don't be bashful in attempting to secure everything on a trade- out basis, for a reduced price basis or for free. Budget $5,500 in seed money to initiate this fund raiser.

Personnel (Staff/Volunteers): An extensive army of volunteers (60-75) and staff (2-5) will make this event a successful annual event. Volunteers should be organized on a committee basis dealing with food, tickets, decoration, promotions, trophies and awards, and the golfing itself. Influential supporters (centers-of-influence) solicit various celebrities to take part in the event and encourage other business and sport people to donate items (trophies, awards, food, etc.) and take out the advertisements on the greens and tees. An outstanding master of ceremony helps to insure a certain level of professionalism or sophistication for the banquet.

RISK MANAGEMENT: Advance planning greatly reduces the greatest risks involved in this fund raiser, that is, failure to secure ticket purchasers and to attract adequate celebrities. Legal liability exposure should be adequately addressed by the general coverage policy of the golf site.

PERMITS/LICENSE: None.

HINTS: The golf tournament could be organized to include one of the following; best ball handicap, best ball scratch, individual handicap and scratch, or even a scramble format. The Calloway system, in which handicaps are given to the players based upon what they scored that particular day, may also be used as an optional format. A skin game could also be incorporated as an option. Once this event is a success subsequent tournaments are easier to plan and implement and are, usually, equally or more successful.

Fund raiser #75
Planned Giving Solicitation

POTENTIAL NET INCOME: $75,000

COMPLEXITY/DEGREE OF DIFFICULTY: High

DESCRIPTION: Potential contributors are approached by representatives of a sport or recreational organization for donations earmarked for a specific purpose. Donors are contacted in person, over the phone and via the mails. Categories of contributions ($50, $100, $500, $1000, $5,000, $10,000, $50,000, etc.) are established so that donors can tailor their individual contributions to fit their budgets. It is very important when implementing this campaign not to overlook the small contributors. The success of this fund raising project rests in securing the contributions from high rollers or heavy hitters as well as the average person within the community. Don't just concentrate on the so-called wealthy segment of the community. Additionally, both the purpose(s) for which the money is being sought (additional lights for the softball fields) and the established financial goal ($75,000) of the fund raising effort are announced at the start of the official fund raising campaign—and should be emphasized throughout the solicitation process of the campaign.

SCHEDULING: The campaign may be initiated at any time of the year. However, the kick-off activities associated with the campaign should coincide with some positive publicity or good news relating to the sponsoring organization. Conversely, no campaign should be initiated during a time when negative publicity surrounds the organization.

RESOURCES:

Facilities: The only facility needed is an office in which meetings may be held, phone calls made and mailings prepared.

Equipment and supplies: The use of a computer, laser printer, word processing and graphics software (desktop publishing), receipt and record books, deposit slips, stationery, envelopes and stamps are all useful tools in the marketing and promotion of the fund raising campaign. Everything printed must be of the highest quality denoting the sophistication of the soliciting organization.

Publicity and promotion: The success of this major project rests upon several factors. First, there must be a recognized need for the solicitation of major sums of money. Second, the organization itself must be viewed in a most favorable light by the general public and, most importantly, by potential donors who possess discretionary monies to contribute. And, third, it is absolutely essential that there be respected and competent individuals able and willing to serve as solicitors of contributions for the Planned Giving Campaign. These individuals (centers of influence) must be held in high esteem by potential donors and must have access or be able to secure access to a wide range of individuals, businesses and organizations capable of contributing money, time, services and/or goods to the campaign. News releases are sent to all news media announcing the kick-off of the Planned Giving Campaign, the names of the individuals comprising the planning committee and the honorary head of the campaign (who should be an important personage within the community). Any really significant or large contributions should always be shared with the media unless the donor objects. Outside the organization's facility should be placed a large wooden display of a thermometer indicating how much money has been raised by the current date. Even area businesses could display signs or posters announcing the financial goals of the campaign.

Time: In some campaigns, the organizers establish a set time period, such as a year, during which solicitation efforts will be made to generate the specified amount of money. However, other organizations do not create any artificial time limit but merely establish a financial goal and continue to work towards that goal until it is reached.

Expenditures: Plan on spending $500 on advertising, mailings, promotion and public relations efforts. The use of computers, printers and appropriate software should be secured on a donated or loan basis.

Personnel (Staff/Volunteers): The foundation of this fund raising effort are the volunteers (25) and staff (2-5) dedicated to making the campaign a success. Securing important individuals who will serve as birddogs in terms of opening doors to potential contributors as well as soliciting donations is imperative. Likewise, establishing an advisory board of knowledgeable persons who will provide appropriate advice as well as provide access to potential contributors is very important. The establishment of a highly respected individual(s) as honorary (co)chairperson(s) of the campaign can work wonders in establishing almost immediate credibility within the community.

RISK MANAGEMENT: There is little downside financial risk nor legal liability exposure in this fund raising effort. Volunteers and staff need to be trained, however, in the art and science of soliciting monies for non-profit entities from both individuals and groups. If there is a major risk involved in this effort it pertains to the actual solicitation activities. There should never be any "hard sell" tactics. Such stratagem runs the risk of alienating the very individuals and organizations that the sponsoring organization is attempting to impress. Remember, negative word of mouth among the community regarding the solicitation efforts can effectively torpedo the Planned Giving Campaign.

PERMITS/LICENSES: No permits or licenses are required with this type of individual, person-to-person, solicitation of funds.

HINTS: It is very important when planning this type of fund raising campaign for the organizers to presolicit a significant percentage of the money being sought (20-25%) before even announcing the existence of the Planned Giving Campaign. In this way, shortly after the announcement of the start of the campaign, within two weeks, the organizing committee is able to publicly announce the successful solicitation of 10% of the total amount being sought. Then, after an additional two or three weeks another very public announcement is made revealing that at the present point in time (4-5 weeks into the campaign) 20% of the goal has been reached. Of course these monies had been contributed/pledged well before the campaign had even be publicized. The important point is that the general public, and potential donors in particular, will view the initial success of the campaign in a most positive light and will be more inclined to contribute to a campaign that is being well supported by others. Similarly, those solicitors seeking donations from individuals, businesses and organizations will be able to point to the tremendous success rate of the campaign as "proof of the pudding" that the purpose(s) for which the money is being sought is recognized as justified and that others within the community are backing the organization's Planned Giving Campaign. People tend to follow others and to emulate their actions. This is true even in the donation of money. Finally, make sure that donors have an easy and convenient method of making their commitments and giving their contributions. Contributions and commitments may be made by cash, checks, credit cards and pledges.

Appendix:

Fundraiser Finder

Title of Fundraising Project	Project Number	Net Profit	Degree of Difficulty/Complexity	Number of People Required	Seed Money Needed	Page
Adopt/Sponsor An Athlete	44	$ 6,000	Low	46-47	$ 250	152
Adult Athletic Walk	62	$ 12,000	High	63-94	$ 400	210
Adult (Co-Ed) Fast-Pitch Softball Tournament	58	$ 10,000	High	27-39	$1,000	195
All You Can Eat Ziti Feast	8	$ 2,000	Moderate	32-39	$ 150	57
Alumni(ae) Athletic Contests	5	$ 1,500	Low	21-40	$ 100	50
Alumni(ae) Athletic Cookout	45	$ 6,000	High	31-37	$ 250	161
"Art in All Media" Auction	11	$ 2,500	Low	11-17	$ 50	65
Bake Sale(s)	1	$ 1,000	Low	5-15	$ 10	40
Barbecue Extravaganza	59	$ 11,000	High	32-54	$1,000	202
Baseball Marathon (100 innings)	64	$ 15,000	High	133	$ 450	215
Boat and RV Show	13	$ 2,500	Low	46-57	$ 300	71
Booster Organization Memberships	63	$ 12,000/yr.	Moderate	10-15	$ 100	212
Breakfast with the Easter Bunny	12	$ 2,500	Moderate	26-31	$ 575	68
Can and Bottle Collection	52	$ 7,500/yr.	Moderate	50-75	$ 50	180
Car Bash	24	$ 3,500	Low	11-12	$ 100	104
Celebrity Golf Tournament	74	$ 26,000	High	62-80	$5,500	242
Celebrity Hockey Game	33	$ 4,000	Moderate	32-34	$ 250	126
Cheerleading Competition	10	$ 2,100	Moderate	15-25	$ 450	63

Co-Educational Invitational Track Extravaganza	69	$ 17,000	High	60-75	$1,000	228
Couch Potato Contest	41	$ 5,500/yr.	Low	6-9	$ 50	152
Custom Bird House Auction	37	$ 4,500	Moderate	50-76	$ 500	137
Day of Game Drawing	56	$ 8,000	Low	10-12	$ 50	190
Day Sport Camp	46	$ 6,000	High	17-26	$ 500	164
Dinner Dance	38	$ 4,500	Moderate	35-40	$ 500	140
Discount "Credit" Cards	39	$ 4,500	Moderate	45-50	$1,500	142
Donkey Basketball Competition	25	$ 3,500	Moderate	20-30	$ 500	106
Doughnuts and Other Pastry Items for Sale	65	$ 15,000/yr.	Moderate	20	$ 50	218
Dunking Booth	26	$ 3,500/yr.	Moderate	11-17	$ 200	109
Endowment Challenge	68	$ 16,000/yr.	High	18-25	$ 300	226
Fall Flower Bulb Sale	27	$ 3,500	Moderate	31-37	$ 100	111
Family Portraits	23	$ 3,400	Low	25-29	$ 200	101
50's Sock Hop	18	$ 3,000	Moderate	37-49	$ 750	85
Fish Fry Fundraising Dinner	28	$ 3,500	Moderate	53-65	$ 250	114
Free Professional Car Wash	47	$ 6,000	Low	25-30	$ 50	167
Gift Box for the Boss	36	$ 4,300	Moderate	31-35	$ 200	134
Great Duck Race	50	$ 7,000	High	52-64	$ 750	174
Hands-On Marathon	14	$ 2,500	Moderate	16-22	$ 50	74
Hole-in-One Contest	42	$ 5,500	Low	26-32	$ 50	154
Home for the Holidays	66	$ 15,000	High	50-75	$1,500	220
Honor Banquet	21	$ 3,100	Moderate	7-13	$ 350	96
Lawn Mower Obstacle Race	48	$ 6,000	Low	22-28	$ 500	169
Marching Band Competition	29	$ 3,500	Moderate	26-36	$ 300	116
Miniature Golf Tournament	34	$ 4,000	Moderate	16-22	$ 350	129
Murder Mystery Dinner Party	30	$ 3,500	Moderate	21-29	$ 240	119
Musical Concert	67	$ 15,000	High	87-105	$2,500	223
National Alumni(ae) Tennis Tournaments	72	$ 20,000	Moderate	25-40	$ 300	236
Pizza Extravaganza	2	$ 1,000	Low	6-9	$ 100	42
Planned Giving Solicitation	75	$ 75,000	High	27-30	$5,000	245
Playground Teen Dance	6	$ 1,500	Moderate	23-24	$ 500	52

Quilt Raffle	19	$ 3,000	Low	27-33	$ 150	88
Race to a Healthy Lifestyle	53	$ 7,500	High	13-20	$ 250	182
Raffle-Auction	20	$ 3,000	Moderate	31-37	$ 50	90
Raffle of a Collectible	31	$ 3,500	Moderate	16-17	$ 150	122
Rock-a-Thon	51	$ 7,450	Low	51-77	$ 50	177
Rodeo Festival	60	$ 11,000	High	52-58	$ 350	204
Singing Valentine	4	$ 1,100	Low	19-26	$ 100	47
Sleigh Rides	49	$ 6,000	Moderate	30-40	$ 450	172
Social Pyramid	54	$ 7,750	Low	155	$ 50	185
Souvenir Sport Paraphernalia Auction	57	$ 10,000	Moderate	30-35	$ 350	192
Spaghetti Supper	35	$ 4,000	Moderate	34-45	$ 500	132
Spell-a-Thon	43	$ 5,500	Low	65-66	$ 100	156
Sport Poster for Sale	17	$ 2,750	Low	31-32	$ 750	82
Square Dance Round-Up	15	$ 2,500	Moderate	29-48	$ 500	76
St. Valentine's Day Dinner Dance	40	$ 5,000	Moderate	22-28	$ 200	145
Stay-At-Home (Pseudo) Extravaganza	9	$ 2,000	Low	21-27	$ 250	60
Take An Athlete to Dinner	7	$ 1,500	Low	10-14	$ 100	55
Taste of the Nations	70	$ 17,000	High	48-55	$ 300	231
Team Banquet	22	$ 3,300	Moderate	26-27	$ 200	98
Thematic Commemorative Event and Dinner	3	$ 1,000	Moderate	26-37	$ 300	45
"There's A Man in the Kitchen" Cookbook	55	$ 7,800	Moderate	32-43	$ 200	187
Three-on-Three (Co-Ed) Basketball Tournament	61	$ 11,000	High	55-67	$ 500	207
Tie-a-Thon	32	$ 3,500	Low	37-54	$ 200	124
Vehicle Donation	71	$ 20,000	Low	13-22	$1,000	234
Weekly Sports Pool	73	$ 25,000	Low	47-58	$1,000	239
Weight Loss Marathon	16	$ 2,500	Moderate	35-37	$ 200	79

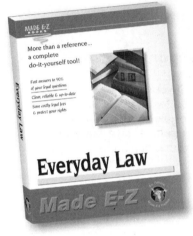

Whatever you need to know, we've made it E-Z!

Informative text and forms you can fill out on-screen.* From personal to business, legal to leisure—we've made it E-Z!

Personal & Family

For all your family's needs, we have titles that will help keep you organized and guide you through most every aspect of your personal life.

Business

Whether you're starting from scratch with a home business or you just want to keep your corporate records in shape, we've got the programs for you.

	ITEM #	QTY.	PRICE‡	EXTENSION
Made E-Z Software				
E-Z Construction Estimator	SS4300		$24.95	
E-Z Contractors' Forms	SS4301		$24.95	
Contractors' Business Builder Software Bundle	SS4002		$49.95	
Corporate Secretary	SS4003		$24.95	
Asset Protection Made E-Z	SS4304		$24.95	
Corporate Records Made E-Z	SS4305		$24.95	
Vital Records Made E-Z	SS4306		$24.95	
Managing Employees	SS4307		$24.95	
Accounting Made E-Z	SS4308		$24.95	
Limited Liability Companies (LLC)	SS4309		$24.95	
Partnerships	SS4310		$24.95	
Solving IRS Problems	SS4311		$24.95	
Winning In Small Claims Court	SS4312		$24.95	
Collecting Unpaid Bills Made E-Z	SS4313		$24.95	
Selling On The Web (E-Commerce)	SS4314		$24.95	
Your Profitable Home Business Made E-Z	SS4315		$24.95	
Get Out Of Debt Made E-Z	SS4317		$24.95	
E-Z Business Lawyer Library	SS4318		$49.95	
E-Z Estate Planner	SS4319		$49.95	
E-Z Personal Lawyer Library	SS4320		$49.95	
Payroll Made E-Z	SS4321		$24.95	
Personal Legal Forms and Agreements	SS4322		$24.95	
Business Legal Forms and Agreements	SS4323		$24.95	
Employee Policies and Manuals	SS4324		$24.95	
Incorporation Made E-Z	SW1176		$24.95	
Last Wills Made E-Z	SW1177		$24.95	
Everyday Law Made E-Z	SW1185		$24.95	
Everyday Legal Forms & Agreements Made E-Z	SW1186		$24.95	
Business Startups Made E-Z	SW1192		$24.95	
Credit Repair Made E-Z	SW2211		$24.95	
Business Forms Made E-Z	SW2223		$24.95	
Buying and Selling A Business Made E-Z	SW2242		$24.95	
Marketing Your Small Business Made E-Z	SW2245		$24.95	
Get Out Of Debt Made E-Z	SW2246		$24.95	
Winning Business Plans Made E-Z	SW2247		$24.95	
Successful Resumes Made E-Z	SW2248		$24.95	
Solving Business Problems Made E-Z	SW 2249		$24.95	
Profitable Mail Order Made E-Z	SW2250		$24.95	
Deluxe Business Forms	SW2251		$49.95	
E-Z Small Business Library	SW2252		$49.95	
Sub-total for Software			$	
Made E-Z Guides				
Bankruptcy Made E-Z	G300		$14.95	
Incorporation Made E-Z	G301		$14.95	
Divorce Made E-Z	G302		$14.95	
Credit Repair Made E-Z	G303		$14.95	
Living Trusts Made E-Z	G305		$14.95	
Living Wills Made E-Z	G306		$14.95	
Last Will & Testament Made E-Z	G307		$14.95	
Buying/Selling Your Home Made E-Z	G311		$14.95	
Employment Law Made E-Z	G312		$14.95	
Collecting Child Support Made E-Z	G315		$14.95	
Limited Liability Companies Made E-Z	G316		$14.95	
Partnerships Made E-Z	G318		$14.95	
Solving IRS Problems Made E-Z	G319		$14.95	
Asset Protection Made E-Z	G320		$14.95	
Buying/Selling A Business Made E-Z	G321		$14.95	
Financing Your Business Made E-Z	G322		$14.95	
Profitable Mail Order Made E-Z	G323		$14.95	
Selling On The Web Made E-Z	G324		$14.95	
SBA Loans Made E-Z	G325		$14.95	
Solving Business Problems Made E-Z	G326		$14.95	
Advertising Your Business Made E-Z	G327		$14.95	
Shoestring Investing Made E-Z	G330		$14.95	
Stock Market Investing Made E-Z	G331		$14.95	
Fund Raising Made E-Z	G332		$14.95	
Money For College Made E-Z	G334		$14.95	
Marketing Your Small Business Made E-Z	G335		$14.95	

‡ *Prices are for a single item, and are subject to change without notice.*

See an item in this book you would like to order?

1. Photocopy this order form.
2. Complete your order and mail to:

MADE E◆Z PRODUCTS

**384 S Military Trail
Deerfield Beach, FL 33442
www.MadeE-Z.com**

Company Purchase Orders welcome
with approved credit.

All orders ship UPS Ground unless
otherwise specified.

continued on next page

	ITEM #	QTY.	PRICE‡	EXTENSION
Owning A No-Cash-Down Business Made E-Z	G336		$14.95	
Offshore Investing Made E-Z	G337		$14.95	
Multi-level Marketing Made E-Z	G338		$14.95	
Get Out Of Debt Made E-Z	G340		$14.95	
Your Profitable Home Business Made E-Z	G341		$14.95	
Winning Business Plans Made E-Z	G342		$14.95	
Mutual Fund Investing Made E-Z	G343		$14.95	
Business Startups Made E-Z	G344		$14.95	
Successful Resumes Made E-Z	G346		$14.95	
Free Stuff For Everyone Made E-Z	G347		$14.95	
Sub-total for Guides			$	
Made E-Z Kits				
Bankruptcy Kit	K300		$24.95	
Incorporation Kit	K301		$24.95	
Divorce Kit	K302		$24.95	
Credit Repair Kit	K303		$24.95	
Living Trust Kit	K305		$24.95	
Living Will Kit	K306		$24.95	
Last Will & Testament Kit	K307		$19.95	
Buying and Selling Your Home Kit	K311		$24.95	
Employment Law Kit	K312		$24.95	
Limited Liability Company Kit	K316		$24.95	
Business Startups Kit	K320		$24.95	
Small Business/Home Business Kit	K321		$24.95	
Sub-total for Kits			$	
Made E-Z Books				
Everyday Legal Forms & Agreements Made E-Z	BK407		$24.95	
Personnel Forms Made E-Z	BK408		$24.95	
Collecting Unpaid Bills Made E-Z	BK409		$24.95	
Corporate Records Made E-Z	BK410		$24.95	
Everyday Law Made E-Z	BK411		$24.95	
Vital Records Made E-Z	BK412		$24.95	
Business Forms Made E-Z	BK414		$24.95	
Sub-total for Books			$	
Labor Law Posters				
☆ Federal Labor Law	LP001		$14.95	
☆ State Specific Labor Law see state listings below			$39.95	

State	Item#	QTY	State	Item#	QTY	State	Item#	QTY
AL	83801		KY	83817		ND	83834	
AK	83802		LA	83818		OH	83835	
AZ	83803		ME	83819		OK	83836	
AR	83804		MD	83820		OR	83837	
CA	83805		MA	83821		PA	83838	
CO	83806		MI	83822		RI	83839	
CT	83807		MN	83823		SC	83840	
DE	83808		MS	83824		S. Dakota not available		
DC	83848		MO	83825		TN	83842	
FL	83809		MT	83826		TX	83843	
GA	83810		NE	83827		UT	83844	
HI	83811		NV	83828		VT	83845	
ID	83812		NH	83829		VA	83846	
IL	83813		NJ	83830		WA	83847	
IN	83814		NM	83831		WV	83849	
IO	83815		NY	83832		WI	83850	
KS	83816		NC	83833				

☆ Required by Federal & State Laws

Sub-total for Posters	$
TOTAL FOR ALL PRODUCTS	$
Add Shipping & Handling $3.50 for first item, $1.50 for each additional item	$
TOTAL PRODUCTS and S & H	$
Florida Residents add 6% sales tax	$
TOTAL OF ORDER	$

‡ Prices are for a single item, and are subject to change without notice.

❋ FOR FASTER SERVICE ❋

Order by phone:
(954) 480-8933

Order by fax:
(954) 480-8906

SS 2001 r3

MADE E-Z™
PRODUCTS

Name

Company

Position

Address

City

State   Zip

Phone
(   )

PAYMENT

❑ check enclosed, payable to:
Made E-Z Products, Inc.
384 S. Military Trail
Deerfield Beach, FL 33442

❑ charge my credit card: ❑ MasterCard ❑ VISA

ACCOUNT NO.   EXP. DATE

Signature: (required for credit card purchases)

Index

A-C ✦✦✦✦

D-M ✦✦✦✦

N-S••••••

T-W••••••